WHAT God SAYS ABOUT MUSIC

Eurydice V. Osterman, D.M.A.

AWSAHM MUSIC, INC.
P. O. Box 3586
Huntsville, AL 35810-0586

Library of Congress Card Number: 97-94873
Osterman, Eurydice V. (Eurydice Valenis)
    What God Says About Music/
    Eurydice V. Osterman
    p. Cm.
    Includes bibliographical references and indices.
    ISBN 0-9661690-0-X
    1. Music   2. Music—Religious aspects.   I. Title
    BV 310.075 1998

TABLE OF CONTENTS

DEDICATION

This book is dedicated to my mother, Ella L. Osterman, for the musical genes that she passed on to me; for the training that she provided; and for all of the prayers, encouragement, and support that she has given me through the years.

ACKNOWLEDGMENTS

I wish to thank those persons who took time out of their busy schedules to help in the production of this book: Dr. Oliver J. Davis, Oakwood College English Department, for expeditiously reading and editing the manuscript; Elder Eric C. Ward, former pastor of the Oakwood College Church, for writing the "Foreword"; Dr. Kenneth Mulzac, Oakwood College Religion and Theology Department, for his invaluable guidance on the details of publishing; Dr. Ella Simmons, Academic Vice President of Oakwood College, for providing me with the environment and the encouragement needed to write and publish this book; Ramona Hyman, Dorothy Patterson, and Karen Tucker, Oakwood College English Department, for helping me to choose an appropriate bibliographic format; Barbara Newton for her suggestions on designing the book cover; Oakwood College Graphixx for designing the book cover and formatting the document; Letitia Cochran and Kerry Holland for their invaluable assistance at the computer; Mr. Morris Iheanacho, librarian, for cataloging the book; Drs. Agniel Samson, Acting Chair of the Oakwood College Religion and Theology Department, and James Doggette for reviewing and critiquing the content; and Dr. John L. Cashin for naming my publishing company—AWSAHM MUSIC (A Wonderful Servant, A Hard Master).

I also wish to thank my family and many friends for their support, encouragement, and prayers throughout this venture.

Most of all, I want to thank GOD for giving me the gift of music, for entrusting me with this task and guiding me each step of the way, and providing the opportunity for me to make a difference.

PREFACE

In 1981 when I was asked to be a presenter at the Regional Youth Congress in Detroit, Michigan, little did I realize that preparing for that event would set in motion the making of this book. From that time on I have conducted music seminars on four continents of the world and have found that the issues and concerns about music are basically the same, notwithstanding race, culture, or denomination. As I researched and studied these issues I began to collect a great deal of information that I felt needed to be published. In 1994 I began the process of compiling the material but, due to numerous responsibilities and other distractions, the project ended up on the "back burner."

Late one evening in October, 1996, as I was coming home from work, God spoke to me (in a voice that I perceived to be quite audible) saying, "finish the book," and, having heard that voice before on several occasions, I obeyed without hesitation. God then created the conditions and the environment necessary for me to write, and from that day to this I have diligently and tenaciously stuck to the task until it was completed, in spite of interference from the enemy. I am so very thankful to have been used as God's instrument in this effort.

Because music is so very complex this book does not purport to have "all the answers," but it does address the most common issues of concern from the Bible (KJV), the Spirit of Prophecy (the writings of Ellen G. White, a prophetess, and one of the founders of the Seventh-day Adventist Church), other Christian authors, and scientific research. Therefore, it is my sincere desire that as you read you, too, will hear God speaking to you through these witnesses, and will be enlightened and edified from the experience.

FOREWORD

By Eric C. Ward, Pastor Emeritus
of the Oakwood College Seventh-day Adventist Church

Dr. Eurydice V. Osterman has served as professor and Chairperson of the Music Department at Oakwood College, a Minister of Music at the Oakwood College Church, organist, and choral director of the church and college choirs for nearly twenty years, and has received numerous awards and citations for her work. Her academic qualifications, keen ability at the instruments, and musical compositions are remembered by her peers, pupils, and the people who worship in our college setting.

What God Says About Music is both Biblical, musical, and vital to Christians of any denomination. First of all, it teaches in a unique way the relationship of music to the Ten Commandments, God's constitution operating in our world and the universe. Secondly, this scholarly work reminds us that the only art we will take from earth to heaven will be the art of music. The book shows us that discovering God's word on music is the basis for discernment; that music is the language of heaven; and that God's word leaves nothing to the imagination nor does it contain any "gray areas."

The author points out the fact that Lucifer, God's greatest church musician, was expelled from heaven because of pride, and shows how he continues to challenge, mock, and belittle God through the tool of music, both secular and pseudo-religious. She also shows that the person of Jesus Christ, not the person or personality of the performer, should be glorified in music. "If one deems sacred music dull and lifeless and needs to be 'livened up' via the profane, he or she has missed the point that the sacred does not need to be sensational to be meaningful." "When we can see Christ in Gethsemane sweating great drops of blood, dying on the cross in agony, self will no longer clamor to be recognized." It is only then

vii

that we will offer to God worship of "fire," not "strange fire," as discussed in the book.

The author shows us that music of the church is not the music of the theater, but represents a place of worship to the only true God. Jesus taught that our motives and attitude (spirit), coupled with Biblical principles (truth), form the basis of true worship. Her work reminds us in positive terms that music in worship is as important as are prayer and the spoken word. And, as a tool for saving souls, it does several things in perfecting character and fighting the inroads of Satan.

The author warns of the "hooks and lines" that are used in commercial music to sell songs instead of substantive lyrics based upon scripture. She says that we need to be aware of "pronoun" songs as well as "crossover" songs, and the effects of subliminal manipulation of words and phrases, an innovation in the religious music world.

The readers are also reminded that the greatest instrument of all is the human voice, created by God Himself, and like all manufacturers, is provided with instruction manuals via His word and the Spirit of Prophecy for proper use, care, and maintenance of the instrument. "A lifetime warranty is guaranteed if the principles are diligently observed. When Christ returns He will require of us an explanation of what, when, where, why, how and for whom this talent and gift was used."

The chapters are short, succinct, and contain balanced expressions of good common Biblical sense. Did God ever recommend the use of drums in Divine Worship? The answer is in Chapter Ten. Was dancing ever used in the Bible for sacred worship? Let Chapter Eleven answer that question. The book stimulates our understanding of music in our DNA, and tells how it affects one's mind and body. This will be found in Chapter Twelve.

The reader will note with appreciation that every major point is fortified with copious contextual statements from the word of God and confirmed by the Spirit of Prophecy.

The book is excellent. It is not boring, but is interesting, enlightening, readable, and profound.

INTRODUCTION

"This is the dawning of the Age of Aquarius." For those old enough to remember, these words are from the hit song recorded in the early 1970's by the group, the Fifth Dimension. Perhaps the message of this song was but a subtle announcement that the stage had been set, and the events leading to the "new world order" were just over the horizon.

Malachi Martin, a former Jesuit and professor at the Vatican's Pontifical Biblical Institute, and an expert on the Catholic Church, says that the new world order is a plan to unite the world and transcend all barriers that now separate cultures and religions. It is about who will establish and control the first one world system of government and hold control over each individual and community, its money, trade, commerce, educational system and the emblems of its national identity.

He went on to say that Pope John II "insists that men have no reliable hope of creating a viable geopolitical system unless it is on the basis of Roman Catholic Christianity" (Martin: 492). On the other hand, George Bush, former President of the United States, felt differently. In his State of the Union address on February 18, 1991, he indicated that only the United States can accomplish this.

On the surface the new world order is a race between the nations for such geopolitical control. However, according to the Bible, the hidden agenda is really a plan devised by Satan that will be implemented through the Catholic ("universal") church, and will use music (the "universal language") as one of its main tools to accomplish this goal.

One way of facilitating the implementation of the new world order is through ecumenism—uniting religions by setting aside theological and ideological differences, and emphasizing elements common to most religions. Today's "religious" music, which I call "generic religious music," appears to follow the same pattern in that it does not define religious or theological beliefs, but focuses on general themes such as praise to God, the love and grace of God, unity, etc. And as "innocent" as they may appear, songs or hymns such as *"Hail, Holy Queen, Enthroned Above"* or *"Never A Dying Soul,"* and other such songs that speak of being in heaven with loved ones, foster the idea of spiritualism—a perpetuation of the lie, *"thou shalt not surely die."* Even the media conditions us to believe this by merging dead souls with live ones in commercial advertisements. Take for instance, Natalie Cole singing with her deceased father, Nat King Cole, and even touching his hand via technology, as if he were still alive; or the late Lucille Ball talking to a sales representative in a Service Merchandise store.

As Seventh-day Adventists, we have been affected by ecumenicism in that we have begun to adopt what we deem to be "innocent" customs and terminology of other denominations. We are told in the Spirit of Prophecy that "when protestantism shall stretch her hand across the gulf to grasp the hand of Roman power, when she shall reach over the abyss to clasp hands with spiritualism. . . then we may know that the time has come for the marvelous working of Satan, and that the end is near" (White: 5T 451).

The beat and feel of today's popular music, which I call *"unicultural,"* has transcended the different cultures and has become the means for breaking down barriers that used to separate them. While traveling in Europe, I recall riding in a taxi in Prague, Czech Republic to the train station. The driver, who could not speak English, seemed to enjoy a song by Michael Jackson that he was listening to on the radio. Although he did not understand the words, he understood the music. As I traveled from country to country, not only in Europe but on other continents as well, I observed that commercial music has indeed broken down many barriers and seems to have made the world smaller; it sounds the same everywhere.

The origin of the new world order can be traced back to the war in heaven between God and Lucifer (See Revelation 12:7, 9, 17). What could possibly have been the cause of this controversy? Why would Lucifer, the most exalted of all the angels, seek to challenge God? Music must have been involved.

Initially, when God created the heaven and the earth, He created two special musical beings—Lucifer, the crowning act of creation in heaven, and human beings, the crowning act of creation on earth. Lucifer was not only able to harmonize with himself vocally, but he was also the orchestra. In Ezekiel 28:14, we find that he was created with "tabrets" and "pipes" (his own percussion section). Therefore, he fully understands the intricacies of music, especially the rhythm and beat and how they affect us physically, mentally, and spiritually.

When God created humans, though not as elaborate as Lucifer, He wrote music into the very fibers of their being. This aspect will be discussed in more detail in Chapter Twelve. Having a knowledge of this, Lucifer became incensed that God would not consult him and include him in the creation of humans; after all, he was the epitome of musical expression. He then raged war in heaven and has sought to mock God and malign His character throughout the universe ever since.

God specifically says that His commandments (the essence of His character) are to be obeyed and should be in our hearts [thoughts] at all times, and that we should diligently teach them to our children and talk of them in the home, when we walk by the way, when we lie down, and when we arise (Deuteronomy 6:7-9). However, Satan has devised numerous ways in which to try to make them null and void. Through the medium of music he has very skillfully and very subtly programmed those who are not on guard to accomplish this goal without them ever realizing it.

The principle behind the first commandment, *"Thou Shalt Have No Other Gods before Me"* (Exodus 20:3) is that of total commitment to God. For those who spend a lot of time listening to music while neglecting personal prayer and bible study, the one to whom we yield ourselves is our god. "Music has occupied the hours which should have been devoted to prayer. Music is the idol which many professed Sabbath-keeping Christians worship. Satan has no objection to music if he can make that a channel through which to gain access to the minds of the youth" (White: 1T 585, 586).

"Jehovah, the eternal, self-existent, uncreated One, Himself the source and sustainer of all, is alone entitled to supreme reverence and worship. Man is forbidden to give to any other object the first place in his affections or his service. Whatever we cherish that tends to lessen our love for God or to interfere with the service due Him, of that do we make a god" (White: PP 305).

The second commandment deals with idolatry. *"Thou shalt not make unto thee any graven image or any likeness of anything that is in the heaven above, or that is in the earth beneath, or that is in the water under the earth:*

Thou shalt not bow down thyself to them nor serve them: for I the Lord thy God am a jealous God, ..." (Exodus 20:4, 5).

Satan entices us to bow down and worship him not only with his music, but through idolizing the artists, many of whom are not Christians or, worse yet, some of whom are gay or lesbian, in spite of the fact that they may sing about Jesus. Purchasing their music and putting their pictures on the wall, or wearing their images on clothing, in essence, condones and supports their lifestyles and habits. "Though in a different form, idolatry exists in the Christian world today as verily as it existed among ancient Israel. . ." (White: GC 511).

"The attempt to represent the Eternal One by material objects would lower man's conception of God. The mind, turned away from the infinite perfection of Jehovah, would be attracted to the creature rather than to the Creator. And as his conceptions of God were lowered, so would man become degraded. . . Idolatry being spiritual adultery, the displeasure of God against it is fitly called jealousy. . . It is inevitable that children should suffer from the consequences of parental wrong-doing, but they are not punished for the parent's guilt, except as they participate in their sins. It is usually the case, however, that children walk in the steps of their parents. . . Wrong tendencies, perverted appetites, and debased morals, as well as physical disease and degeneracy, are transmitted as a legacy from father to son, to the third and fourth generation. . . And those who are faithful in His service, mercy is promised. . ." (White: PP 306).

"Thou shalt not take the name of the Lord thy God in Vain, for the Lord will not hold him guiltless that taketh His name in vain" (Exodus 20:7). This commandment deals with mixing the holy with the profane. This not only applies to using God's name in profanity, but verbalizing God's name in music which does not necessarily mean that it is glorified. Before the late 1960s it was easy to distinguish sacred from secular music. Today, however, it is difficult to do so because it has become so commercialized.

Many are deluded into believing that if the music is classified as *"religious"* it is alright to listen to it or perform it. They do not realize that not all religious music is "good." We must be ever mindful that for every original Satan has his counterfeit. As a matter of fact, although we use the terms "Christian" or religious interchangeably, there is a difference between the two. By comparison, Christian music is *spiritual*, elevating, refining, and appealing to both the intellect and the emothions. It directs the focus of attention toward God. It fosters commitment to duty and obedience to God's commandments. Religious music is a generic, commercial product that is primarily concerned with sales, not souls. It is shallow and superficial, and tends to minimize one's responsibility and duty to obey God's requirements. Whereas Christian music glorifies God and puts the focus upon Him, commercial religious music does not, but instead tends to glorify the performer.

An article written by Richard Harrington, correspondent for the Washington Post, says that the religious record industry has recognized the "untapped audiences" for "positive pop" by seizing to capitalize upon the opportunity to make big sales by fusing current popular sounds with religious words. He also referred to a statement by John Styll, editor of "Contemporary Christian Music Magazine," who said that "the record companies realize they are dealing with a commercial product and they have to consider the entertainment factor of the record. The message may be great, but unless the framework is well executed, people are not going to listen to it" (Harrington: HT 1C). God has not changed his requirements to make salvation more marketable. The pure gospel must be free of such adulteration. "By the frequent and thoughtless repetition of His name, we dishonor Him. All should meditate upon His majesty, and His purity, and holiness, that the heart may be impressed with a sense of His exalted character; and His holy name should be uttered with reverence and solemnity" (White: PP 306).

"Remember the sabbath day to keep it holy. . . ." (Exodus 20:8). The Sabbath is the issue over which we will either receive the mark of the beast or the seal of God, and the way in which we now observe it is a test of our allegiance to God. By observing the seventh day as a day of worship we acknowledged Him as Creator of the universe, and that He is worthy of our praise and adoration.

When it comes to worship the enemy makes it very difficult for us to focus our attention upon God by creating distractions that shift our attention to other things. For instance, there are some who tend to base their Sabbath *"blessing"* upon whoever sings, plays, or speaks. This expectation seems to have created an environment for entertainment, and in many cases, the music that worshippers enjoy so much is nothing more than an aural stimulant that is mistaken for the working of the Holy Spirit. It is no wonder that, over the years, the church has literally been transformed from a congregation into an audience, and instead of leading minds to remember God, this often causes them to forget Him. "Satan is determined, if possible, to intermingle with religious services his evil influences. Let there be no theatrical display, for this will not help to strengthen belief in the Word of God. Rather, it will divert attention to the human instrument. . . ." (White: TDG 359).

"Honor thy father and thy mother that thy days may be long upon the land which the Lord thy God giveth thee" (Exodus 20:12). This is the only commandment containing a promise of longevity because God knew that if left unchecked, rebellion and disrespect for parents lead to disrespect for civil authority, and ultimately disrespect for God. In many homes, music is a cause of rebellion and disrespect for parents. Once, while speaking with a parent, I noticed a gash upon his forehead. He said that his son struck him during an argument over the type of music he was listening to. Unfortunately, this scenario is very common. "He who rejects the rightful authority of his parents, is rejecting the authority of God. . . It also enjoins respect for ministers and rulers, and for all others to whom God has delegated authority . . . ." (White: PP 306).

"Thou shalt not kill" (Exodus 20:13). The body is the *"temple of God."* However, Satan uses *his* music in an attempt to defile and ultimately destroy it. Today's music contains elements (lyrics, beat, volume, etc.) that are not only harmful to the physical body, but also have the potential of destroying the spiritual temple. This will be discussed in more detail in Chapter Twelve. "The spirit of hatred and revenge [as is characteristic of much of today's pop music], or the indulgence of any passion that leads to injurious acts toward others, or causes us even to wish them harm; a selfish neglect of caring for the needy or suffering; all self-indulgence or unnecessary deprivation or excessive labor that tends to injure health, all these are, to a greater or less degree, violations of the sixth commandment" (White: PP 308).

"Thou shalt not commit adultery" (Exodus 20:14). Today, the #1 selling agent is sex. Sex is used to sell cars, clothes, toothpaste, and yes, even religious music. If you pick up any newspaper or magazine, or listen to any news report, or any television show, the basic theme is a reflection of what is in the lyrics of most of today's popular music—sex! Society is literally acting out what it constantly feeds upon and is subliminal-

ly being trained to break down its moral values through music. "This commandment forbids not only acts of impurity, but sensual thoughts and desires, or any practice that tends to excite them. Purity is demanded not only in the outward life, but in the secret intents and emotions of the heart" (White: PP 308).

"Thou shalt not steal." (Exodus 20:15). There are those who will not pay an honest tithe, but yet will pay whatever the cost to attend a concert or to purchase the latest CD, tape, poster, or T-shirt of an admired artist. By spending most of our time and means on music we not only rob God of His time with us, but of the means he has given us in which to spread the gospel. "Both public and private sins are included in this prohibition. . . It declares that every attempt to advantage one's self by the ignorance, weakness, or misfortune of another, is registered in the books of heaven" (White: PP 308).

"Thou shalt not bear false witness. . . ." (Exodus 20:16). To say that a song is "sacred" when in fact the nuances of the music, the beat, and even some of the lyrics imply sensuality is indeed bearing a false witness. This is a common occurrence in crossover songs of "religious pop music". Take for instance, phrases like "no one can love me like you do," "I need your love," or "you bring your love to keep me warm." Songs like these have reduced God's pure and holy love (agape) to mere human eroticism. If the lyrics and the character of the music do not reflect the principles of Christianity then they indeed bear a false witness. "An intention to deceive is what constitutes falsehood. . . Every hint or insinuation calculated to convey an erroneous or exaggerated impression, even the statement of facts in such a manner as to mislead, is falsehood" (White: PP 308).

"Thou shalt not covet. . . ." (Exodus 20:17). Satan wants us to take our eyes off Jesus by distracting us with aspirations for wealth and fame while he stealthily seeks to capture our souls. The glitter and glamour of the music world has caused some to abandon Christian principles in order to enjoy these pleasures for a season. The question then is whether or not our choice of music lessens our desire to be like Christ and represent Him in our dress, diet, associates, and lifestyle. "The tenth commandment strikes at the very root of all sins, prohibiting the selfish desire, from which springs the sinful act" (White: PP 308).

Summary

What role does your choice of music play in the scenario of the new world order? Are you bowing to the beast unawares? When Christ returns to claim His "peculiar" people, what role will your choice of music have played in the salvation of your soul? Since music is the only art that we will take from this earth to heaven, God has not left us in the dark on this issue. He has given us His Word, the Holy Spirit, and the Spirit of Prophecy to guide us in making decisions that will impact upon our eternal destiny. The choice is ours.

CHAPTER ONE

DISCOVERING GOD'S WORD

The battle for our souls is being won or lost in our minds. The issue in this battle between good and evil is that of worship, and music is the tool that Satan is effectively using to gain access to our souls. As a result, he has created such controversy and confusion over the issues pertaining to worship and music until many have adopted the belief that choices in these areas are a "personal thing" and therefore, they are at liberty to choose that which suits their tastes.

God, however, is not silent when it comes to issues on worship and music. Upon careful and prayerful examination of the scriptures, and the Spirit of Prophecy, one will see that He is very articulate in regard to these issues. If He could foresee the need of a plan of salvation, surely He looked down through the annals of time and saw that music would be an issue in the battle for our souls.

Unlike the birds and crickets, and other creatures to which He gave a "fixed" song, God, in His love, has given to man the ability to create his own music, and the power to choose whether or not to render songs of praise and thanksgiving to Him.

In order to remove all doubt as to what is acceptable to Him, God could have easily revealed His will regarding music and worship in a single chapter or book of the Bible as He did the ten commandments, but He chose not to. Instead, He has given infallible principles throughout His Word that govern and transcend chronological, ethnic, cultural, and generational issues of concerns. Thus, it is only through His Word, the Spirit of Prophecy, and the guidance of the Holy Spirit that we can discern His will. **GOD SAYS. . .**

Deuteronomy 10:12,13	*"And now, Israel, what doth the Lord thy God require of thee, but to fear the Lord thy God, to walk in all his ways, and to love him, and to serve the Lord thy God with all thy heart and with all thy soul, to keep the commandments of the Lord, and his statutes. . . ."*
Proverbs 4:7	*"Wisdom is the principal thing; therefore get wisdom: and with all thy getting, get understanding."*
Isaiah 1:18	*"Come now, let us reason together, saith the Lord. . . ."*
Isaiah 8:20	*"To the law and to the testimony: if they speak not according to this word, it is because there is no light in them."*
Isaiah 28:10	*"For precept must be upon precept; line upon line; here a little and there a little."*
Hosea 4:6	*"My people are destroyed for a lack of knowledge . . ."*
Micah 6:8	*"He hath shewed thee, O man, what is good; and what doth the Lord require of thee, but to do justly, and to love mercy, and to walk humbly with thy God?"*
Matthew 5:6	*"Blessed are they which do hunger and*

thirst after righteousness: for they shall be filled."

John 5:39 *"Search the scriptures. . . . they are they which testify of me."*

John 14:26 *"The Comforter. . . . shall teach you all things. . . ."*

1 Corinthians 2:14 *"The natural man receiveth not the things of the Spirit of God. . . . they are spiritually discerned."*

1 Corinthians 3:19 *"For the wisdom of this world is foolishness with God. . . ."*

Colossians 2:8 *"Beware lest any man spoil you through philosophy and vain deceit, after the tradition of men, after the rudiments of the world, and not after Christ."*

James 1:5 *"If any of you lack wisdom, let him ask of God that giveth to all men liberally, and upbraideth not, and it shall be given him."*

"The Holy Spirit is present with the earnest searcher. His illumination shines upon the Word, stamping the truth upon the mind with a new, fresh importance. The searcher is filled with a sense of peace and joy never before felt. The preciousness of truth is realized as never before. A new, heavenly light shines upon the Word, illuminating it as though every letter were tinged with gold. God Himself has spoken to the mind and heart, making the Word spirit and life. Every true searcher of the word lifts his heart to God, imploring the aid of the Spirit. And he soon discovers that which carries him above all the fictitious statements of the would-be teacher, whose weak, tottering theories are not sustained by the Word of the living God" (White: 2SM 39).

"If you had more knowledge you could discern between the spurious and the genuine, the holy and that appointed to utter ruin" (White: 5T 572).

"The carnal mind cannot comprehend these mysteries. If questioners and doubters continue to follow the great deceiver, the impressions and convictions of God's spirit will grow less and less, the promptings of Satan more frequent, until the mind will fully submit to his control. . . . Then that which appears to these bewildered minds as foolishness will be the power of God, and that which God regards as foolishness will be to them the strength of wisdom" (White: 4T 585).

"God does not compel men to give up their unbelief. Before them are light and darkness, truth and error. It is for them to decide which they will accept. The human mind is endowed with power to discriminate between right and wrong. God designs that men shall not decide from impulse, but from weight of evidence, carefully comparing scripture with scripture. . . . The preaching and teaching of His word is one of the means that God has given for diffusing light: but we must bring every man's teaching to the test of Scripture. Whoever will prayerfully study the Bible, desiring to know the truth, that he may obey it, will receive divine enlightenment. He will understand the Scriptures. 'If any man willeth to do His will, he shall know of the teaching'" (White: DA 263).

Summary

Music is the language of heaven, and for this reason, God's Word leaves nothing to the imagination on this subject. The answers to the many "gray areas" may appear to be "ambiguous" only because He has chosen to reveal them to those who will earnestly and diligently seek to find them. He has given guidance on how to go about discovering His will so that we may be able to apply these principles to our lives. We have not been left in the dark about anything that is important to God.

CHAPTER TWO

THE PURPOSE OF MUSIC

Music has many functions for us as individuals. For some it is a profession, while others use it for personal enjoyment, or maybe to help lighten the burden of work, or to pass the time away. Music is important to God because it forms a part of the worship that is continuously rendered unto him in heaven. In addition to this, scripture even records the various circumstances and situations under which music was used.

As Christians, we use music to express praise and adoration to God, and to help impress spiritual truths upon the heart. To this **GOD SAYS. . .**

Psalm 96:2, 3

"Sing unto the Lord, bless his name. . . Declare his glory among the heathen, his wonders among all people."

Psalm 105:1-5

"O give thanks unto the Lord; call upon his name: make known his deeds among the people. Sing unto him, sing psalms unto him: talk ye of all His wondrous works. Glory ye in his holy name: let the heart of

> them rejoice that seek the Lord. Seek the Lord,
> and his strength: seek his face evermore.
> Remember his marvelous works that He hath
> done; his wonders, and the judgments of his
> mouth;"

Psalm 150:1　　　　　"Praise ye the Lord. . . ."

Ephesians 5:19　　　　"Speaking to yourselves in psalms and hymns
> and spiritual songs, singing and making
> melody in your heart to the Lord;"

The Spirit of Prophecy tells us that "Music was made to serve a holy purpose, to lift the thoughts to that which is pure, noble, and elevating, and to awaken in the soul devotion and gratitude to God. What a contrast between the ancient custom and the uses to which music is now too often devoted! How many employ this gift to exalt self, instead of using it to glorify God! A love for music leads the unwary to unite with world lovers in pleasure gatherings where God has forbidden His children to go. Thus, that which is a great blessing when rightly used, becomes one of the most successful agencies by which Satan allures the mind from duty and from the contemplation of eternal things" (White: PP 594).

"There are few means more effective for fixing His words in the memory than repeating them in song. And such song has wonderful power. It has power to subdue rude and uncultivated natures; power to quicken thought and awaken sympathy, to promote harmony of action, and to banish the gloom and foreboding that destroy courage and weaken effort. The value of song as a means of education should never be lost sight of. Let there be singing in the home, of songs that are sweet and pure, and there will be fewer words of censure and more of cheerfulness and hope and joy. Let there be singing in the school, and the pupils will be drawn closer to God, to their teachers and to one another" (White: Ed 167, 168).

"The melody of song is one of God's instrumentalities in the work of saving souls. All the service should be conducted with solemnity and awe, as if in the visible presence of the Master of assemblies" (White: 5T 493).

"I saw singing to the glory of God often drove [away] the enemy, and praising God would beat him back and give us the victory" (White: 3SM 332).

"When Christ was a child like these children here, He was tempted to sin, but He did not yield to temptation. As He grew older He was tempted, but the songs His mother had taught Him to sing came into His mind, and He would lift His voice in praise. And before His companions were aware of it, they would be singing with Him. God wants us to use every facility which Heaven has provided for resisting the enemy" (White: Ev 498).

Summary

Although music serves many purposes in our lives, its function for us as Christians is to serve as a vehicle by which we may glorify God, whether or not the music is sacred or secular. This point will be discussed in more detail in Chapter Thirteen. It is also an effective tool which we can use to impress spiritual truths upon our hearts and to direct our focus upward. Knowing that the enemy of our souls is out to destroy us, the church, sacred music, and everything else associated therewith, we then must be careful of our musical choices, being ever mindful of God's original intent for its function and purpose within our lives.

CHAPTER THREE

THE SOURCE OF THE PROBLEM

The underlying issue of the three angels' messages in Revelation 14 is that of worship. Because of Satan's desire to *"be like the Most High,"* he has, throughout the history of the world, sought to ascribe unto himself the worship, glory, and praise that belong only to God, Creator of heaven and earth. He even tempted Jesus in the wilderness in an effort to try to validate the legitimacy of worshiping him, the "god of this world," but thanks be to God, he failed! To emphasize the corruption and deceitfulness found within him **GOD SAYS...**

Isaiah 14:12-14

> *"How art thou fallen from heaven, O Lucifer, son of the morning! how art thou cut down to the ground, which didst weaken the nations! For thou has said in thine heart, I will ascend into heaven, I will exalt my throne above the stars of God: I will sit also upon the mount of the congregation . . . above the heights of the clouds; I will be like the most High."*

"The experience of the past will be repeated. In the future, Satan's superstitions will assume new forms. Errors will be presented in a pleasing and flattering manner. False theories, clothed with garments of light, will be presented to God's people. Thus Satan will try to deceive, if possible, the very elect. The most seducing influences will be exerted; minds will be hypnotized" (White: 8T 293). In conjunction with this warning **GOD SAYS...**

2 Corinthians 4: 4	*"The god of this world hath blinded the minds of them which believe not, lest the light of the glorious gospel of Christ, who is the image of God, should shine unto them."*
2 Corinthians 11:14	*"For Satan himself is transformed into an angel of light."*
Ephesians 6:12	*"For we wrestle not against flesh and blood, but against principalities, against powers, against the rulers of the darkness of this world, against spiritual wickedness in high places."*
Revelation 12:17;19:10	*"And the dragon was wroth with the woman, and went to make war with the remnant of her seed, which keep the commandments of God and have the testimony of Jesus Christ. . . the testimony of Jesus is the spirit of prophecy."*

Satan has devised numerous counterfeits to deceive us into worshiping him, especially the youth. He camouflages his schemes by trying to divert our attention to controversial issues (generation gap, ethnic and cultural preferences, class or social preferences, gender, etc.) that prove to be divisive and yet, really have nothing to do with our salvation at all. Music is one of his most effective tools. Consider how it is used to create division between youth and age. Young people have a natural tendency to identify with "up-beat" music which has fast tempos and a driving beat compared to those persons one or two generations removed (slow sensual music has its adverse effects as well). Despite the recency or length of a conversion experience, young people are not as mature in making judgements and decisions, spiritual or otherwise, simply because they have not lived as long. The music and recording industry are cognizant of this situation and have capitalized upon the opportunity to make millions of dollars by fusing the current popular sounds with religious words.

And yet, this has become the cherished idol of many a professed Christian. "Anything which tends to absorb the mind and divert it from God assumes the form of an idol. The true and living God is crowded out of the thoughts and the heart, and the soul-temple is defiled by the worship of other gods before the Lord" (White: 4T 632).

"Music has occupied the hours which should have been devoted to prayer. Music is the idol which many professed Sabbath-keeping Christians worship. Satan has no objection to music if he can make that a channel through which to gain access to the minds of the youth. . . When turned to good account, music is a blessing; but it is often made one of Satan's most attractive agencies to ensnare souls. When abused, it leads the unconsecrated to pride, vanity, and folly. When allowed to take the place of devotion and prayer, it is a terrible curse" (White: 1T 585,586). To this **GOD SAYS. . .**

Exodus 20:3   *"Thou shalt have no other gods before me."*

Ezekiel 14:3   *"These men have set up idols in their heart, and put the stumbling block of their iniquity before their face. . . ."*

Matthew 5:9   *"But in vain they do worship me, teaching for doctrine the commandments of men."*

It is a proven fact that when we worship God in this light the result will be reflected not only in our lives but also in our choice of music. Whether young or old, it is only as one grows and matures in Christ that one's musical tastes will become tempered and refined.

Religious music, as stated previously, is a commercial product, and is the *counterfeit* of sacred music. It glorifies the performer, appeals to the carnal nature, and gratifies the senses. Worse yet, the line of distinction between the holy and the profane becomes blurred or even disappears (this issue will be discussed in more detail in the next chapter). More often than not, the message of the music (carnal) and the message of the words (spiritual) are in conflict, which is tantamount to a husband saying "I love you, darling," while physically abusing his wife. This same contradiction can also manifest itself in the spiritual life. Paul described this scenario through his own experience when he said. . .

Romans 7:23	*"But I see another law within my members, warring against the law of my mind, and bringing me into captivity to the law of sin which is in my members."*
Galatians 5:17, 18	*"For the flesh lusteth against the Spirit, and the Spirit against the flesh: and these are contrary the one to the other: so that ye cannot do the things that ye would."*

"Satan is ever on the alert to deceive and mislead. He is using every enchantment to allure men into the broad road of disobedience. He is working to confuse the senses with erroneous sentiments, and remove the landmarks by placing his false inscription over the signposts which God has established to point the right way" (White: OHC 92).

"God requires his servants to walk in the light and not cover their eyes that they may not discern the working of Satan. They should be prepared to warn and reprove those who are in danger through his subtlety. . . [But] instead of resisting the devil that he may flee from them, many are inclined to make a compromise with the powers of darkness" (White: 7T 196).

Summary

"For we wrestle not against flesh and blood, but against principalities, against powers, against the rulers of the darkness of this world, against spiritual

wickedness in high places" (Ephesians 6:12).

Lucifer, God's greatest musical creation, was kicked out of heaven because of his pride, and he has been on the war path ever since, challenging God's character, and seeking to mock Him through His most prized possession—humanity. Music has been one of his most effective tools in accomplishing this. He has crafted and custom-made a counterfeit for every original that God has established, even to the very symbol that will determine our eternal destiny—God's seal, his mark. When we can see the great controversy for what it really is and are able to relate to the ultimate sacrifice of Jesus Christ in our behalf, we will not allow ourselves to become pawns in the hands of the enemy. We must earnestly pray for power to resist him. We must *"be sober, be vigilante; because [our] adversary the devil, as a roaring lion, walketh about, seeking whom he may devour"* (1 Peter 5:8).

CHAPTER FOUR

MIXING THE HOLY
WITH THE PROFANE

True or false; dark or light; strong or weak—these are opposites that, by their very nature, do not mix. The same is true when it comes to the holy and the profane. However, the reality of the fact is that this line of distinction has become blurred, and, as a result of the Laodicean state into which we have fallen, that which is dark is called light, and that which is light is called dark. It has come to the point that it is purely a matter of perception.

In trying to put this issue in the proper perspective, I began to ponder the meaning of the word "holy", so I decided to consult a thesaurus which listed synonyms such as God-fearing; blessed; consecrated; godly; righteous; sacred; and spiritual. Then I asked myself "does our sacred music really portray these characteristics?" But more important, "are these attributes reflected in my life? Are they reflected in your life?"

God wants that which is associated with Him to be different from the world, but today, that is not always the case. When it comes to spiritual matters, things have changed anywhere from the manner in which a service is conducted down to the attire, to say nothing of the music. Today, many protestant churches are now including commercial music and other gimmicks in their "contemporary" (sometimes called "alternative") worship services to attract more people and increase church membership, while efforts to promote and encourage spirituality seem to have become secondary. Thus this "form of godliness" becomes counterproductive. "There is always danger, when the common is mingled with the sacred, that the common will be allowed to take the place of the sacred... When objectionable matter is mingled with sacred matter ... [God's] blessing cannot rest upon the work done" (White: 8T 88).

The music industry has capitalized upon this situation and has produced its own brand of "religious" music that is purely concerned with sales, not souls. It has studied for years the cultural lifestyles and purchasing patterns of individuals, and has skillfully marketed its products to specific groups and subgroups within society. One of its greatest successes has been "crossover songs"—religious love songs that create and influence romantic and sexual fantasies. In essence, these songs mock God's love (agape) and reduce it to human romanticism and passion (eros). "There is a strange abandonment of principle, a lowering of the standard of morality... Never should the mark of distinction between the followers of Jesus and followers of Satan be obliterated" (White: 5T 601,602).

Music that has a worldly association benumbs the mind by appealing to the carnal nature, and hence, evokes physical reactions that minimize the intellectual contemplation that is necessary to discern and understand spiritual precepts. Webster defines *"association"* as being "something linked in memory to imagination with a thing or person that forms a mental bond between sensations, ideas, or memories." To illustrate, when the names Louis Armstrong, Ella Fitzgerald, or Duke Ellington, are mentioned, the mind automatically associates these names with a specific style or genre of musical sound called jazz. Conversely, when the names Bach, George Beverly Shea, or the Rolling Stones are mentioned, the mind automatically associates those names with Baroque, sacred, and rock music respectively, and neither the sound, genre, nor the source can be separated one from the other.

These musical styles have their own environment with which they are associated, and are deemed inappropriate when out of context. For example, a church, a circus, a funeral parlor, or a discotheque all create their own mood, atmosphere, behavior, and music characteristic of the environment. To hear funeral music at a circus or disco music at a funeral would be highly inappropriate and out of order. But yet, this is the case with church music. To illustrate, if the hymn, *Just When I Need Him Most*, is performed in the style of Duke Ellington, it is clearly jazz, which, not only changes the meaning of the song, but worse yet, it mocks God because it bears no resemblance to the attributes of His character as listed above.

The spirit and the character of the music are also suggestive of the mood and the behavior it will engender. For example, if a trumpet trio were to play certain chords in a festive rhythm, as in the introduction of the hymn, *"God of Our Fathers,"* the spirit and the character of that sound would suggest majesty and splendor. Conversely, if a pianist were to softly play a progression of sustained chord clusters in the lower register of the keyboard, slowly and deliberately, the spirit and the character of that sound might suggest mystery, sadness, or even fear.

The sensationalism of the profane will not produce spirituality. If spirituality is indeed the goal, then the mind must be guarded and kept from any influence that would lead it in the wrong direction. Our thoughts reflect the character of the food provided for the mind. Therefore, it should not feed upon music that will weaken the mental powers and stunt spiritual growth. "There will be a growing tendency to place the sacred and the eternal on a level with common things, and those professing the truth will be an offense to God and a disgrace to religion" (White: 5T 500). To this **GOD SAYS. . .**

Leviticus 10:10	*"Put [a] difference between [the] holy and unholy . . . ."*
Joshua 24:14-15	*"And serve him in sincerity and in truth. . . choose you this day whom ye will serve. . . ."*
1 Kings 18:21	*"How long halt ye between two opinions? If the LORD be God, follow him: but if Baal, then follow him."*
Ezekiel 44:5-7, 9, 23	*"And the LORD said. . . mark well, and behold with thine eyes, and hear with thine ears all that I say unto thee concerning all*

the ordinances of the house of the LORD, and all the laws thereof; and mark well the entering in of the house, with every going forth of the sanctuary. . . Say to the rebellious, . . . , ye have brought into my sanctuary strangers, uncircumcised in heart, and uncircumcised in flesh, to be in my sanctuary, to pollute it . . . No stranger, uncircumcised in heart, nor uncircumcised in flesh, shall enter into my sanctuary. . . Teach my people the difference between the holy and profane, and cause them to discern between the unclean and clean."

Matthew 6:24

"No man can serve two masters: for either he will hate the one, and love the other; or else he will hold to the one, and despise the other. Ye cannot serve God and mammon."

Matthew 7:16,18

"Ye shall know them by their fruits. . . a good tree cannot bring forth evil fruit, neither can a corrupt tree bring forth good fruit."

Matthew 22:21

"Render therefore unto Caesar the things which are Caesar's; and unto God the things that are God's."

2 Corinthians 6:17

"Come out from among them and be ye separate, . . . and touch not the unclean thing, and I will receive you. . . ."

James 3:11-12

"Doth a fountain send forth at the same place sweet water and bitter?. . . so can no fountain both yield salt water and fresh."

Just because a style of music is popular does not necessarily mean that it is sacred. As with Nadab and Abihu, God will not accept the "strange fire" of the profane, no matter how attractive and sensational the packaging. He will be glorified as He deserves—on His own terms. We must be ever mindful that the war between good and evil is over the issue of whom we will worship. Mixing the holy with the profane is merely the creation of a situation in which Satan can use us as pawns to mock God, and fool us into believing that we are actually glorifying Him.

"[Satan] planned to work through his human agencies in the religious world, by imbuing them with his own enmity against the champion of truth. He would lead them to reject Christ and to make His life as bitter as possible, hoping to discourage Him in His mission. And the leaders in Israel became instruments of Satan in warring against the Savior" (White: DA 106).

Summary

If one possesses the attitude that sacred music is dull and lifeless, and in need of being "livened up" via the profane, that is a clear indication of the spiritual condition of the heart. That which is sacred is not intended to be sensational. "Let the repenting sinner fix his eyes upon the Lamb of God, which taketh away the sin of the world; and by beholding, he becomes changed. . . . When we behold Him in Gethsemane, sweating great drops of blood, and on the cross dying in agony; when we see this, self will no longer clamor to be recognized" (White: DA 252).

"*Be not deceived, God is not mocked. . . .*" (Galatians 6:7). "*He hath showed thee, o man, what is good, and what doth the Lord require of thee . . .*" (Micah 6:8). Obey or disobey; salvation or damnation; life or death. These opposites represent the choices that will ultimately affect our eternal destiny. Which do you choose?

CHAPTER FIVE

WORLDLINESS

Worldliness is defined as "that which is devoted to this world and its pursuits rather than to religious or spiritual affairs." Worldliness, then, would be the preoccupation with wealth, materialism, commercialism, fame, entertainment, fashion, sensuality, etc., all of which are associated in some way with today's music, both sacred and secular. It stands to reason that to bring anything into the church that is tainted with "worldliness" is inappropriate.

While perusing a Christian magazine, David Wilkerson, a Christian author, described in his book his state of horror and shock when he saw a picture of a "heavy metal" group calling themselves Christians, dressed in the same kind of black leather, nail-studded belts, bracelets, chains, and punk hair style as the twelve sadomasochists who nearly accosted him on the streets of San Francisco. How could this be, he wondered? How could a "Christian" group look and dress like sadomasochists, play their kind of music, and yet call themselves ambassadors of Christ? (See Wilkerson: 84-86)

There is an axiom that says "if it looks like a duck, if it walks like a duck, and if it quacks like a duck, it must be a duck." By the same token, if one thinks like the world, dresses like the world, and behaves like the world, then one must be of the world, for by his fruits one is known. "Eternal things have faded from the mind as of minor consequence, while worldliness has come in like a flood. The great question is: How can I make money?" (White: 5T 261)

One aspect of worldliness that has subtly crept into the church is that of entertainment, the purpose of which is to amuse and captivate the attention in a pleasant, religious manner. It tends to stymie spiritual contemplation, corrupt principle, and weaken intellectual and moral powers. It opens the channel for Satan to sow evil seeds of vanity and self-gratification. Not that this is the motive of today's music in worship, but it is the *result*. The influence of television and the music and record industry have had a tremendous impact upon the consumer. "It is a law of the human mind that by beholding we become changed. Man will rise no higher than his conceptions of truth, purity, and holiness. If the mind is never exalted above the level of humanity, if it is not uplifted to contemplate infinite wisdom and love, the man will be constantly sinking lower and lower" (White: PP 91). To this **GOD SAYS...**

Deuteronomy 14:2   *"For thou art an holy people unto the LORD thy God, and the LORD has chosen thee to be a peculiar people unto himself, above all the nations that are upon the earth."*

Romans 12:2   *"And be not conformed to this world: but be ye transformed by the renewing of your mind. . . ."*

2 Corinthians 4:4   *"The god of this world hath blinded the minds of them which believe not. . . ."*

Colossians 3:2   *"Set your affection on things above, not on things on the earth."*

Titus 2:12   *"Denying ungodliness and worldly lusts, we should live soberly, righteously, and godly, in this present world."*

James 1:27   *"Pure religion and undefiled before God and the Father is this, . . . to keep himself unspotted from the world."*

James 4:4   *"Know ye not that the friendship of the world is enmity with God? whosoever therefore will be a friend of the world is the enemy of God."*

I John 2:15   *"Love not the world, neither the things that are in the world. If any man love the world, the love of the Father is not in him."*

1 John 5:21   *"Little children, keep yourselves from idols. Amen."*

Unfortunately, commercialism has had an impact upon the way music is rendered nowadays; it has transformed the church from a place of worship into a theater. The focus of attention is placed upon the musician(s) rather than upon God, and the congregation, now relegated to a sedentary existence, has turned into an *audience of spectators.* "Let all who are connected with the service of God be guarded, lest by desire for display they lead others into indulgence and self-glorification. . . There should be in the [worship] nothing of a theatrical nature. . . It is not safe for anyone of you to bring into his presence a marred sacrifice, a sacrifice that costs neither study nor prayer. Such an offering [God] cannot accept" (White: 7T 90, 115, 190). Another occasion on which the congregation is unable to participate in the service is when the scripture reading is taken from a different version of the Bible. A solution to this problem is to print the text in the bulletin if a different version of the Bible is used.

This trend of congregational spectating can be traced back to the Dark Ages when the laity, deemed to be lower than the clergy, had to observe and comply with the dictates of the clergy. This was not God's idea of worship by any means, but an invention of the enemy. One way to prevent this from happening is to involve the congregation in singing as often as possible. When the voice of each individual is raised in song, the enthusiasm becomes contagious and will drive the enemy away. "In the meetings held, let a number be chosen to take part in the song service. And let the singing be accompanied with music instruments skillfully handled. The singing is not always to be done by a few. As often as possible, let the entire congregation join" (White: 9T 144).

"When the Lord requires us to be distinct and peculiar, how can we crave popularity or seek to imitate the customs and practices of the world? We are to elevate our standard just a little above the world's standard, but we are to make the distinction decidedly apparent. The reason we have had so little influence upon unbelieving relatives and associates is that there has been so little decided difference between our practices and those of the world" (White: 6T 143, 146).

Therefore, we must be ever vigilant and aware of the subtle ways in which worldliness can creep into the church. For if we give the enemy an inch he will surely take a mile.

Summary

The sensual gratification that is so pleasing to the multitudes is the noxious vapor of worldliness (via entertainment), disguised as a "form of godliness" ("praise to the Lord" and other accolades), that is paralyzing the church and sending it further into a Laodicean state of being. It is interesting to note that Satan tempted Jesus with these same worldly elements. Our only recourse is to shun everything that exalts the false and superficial above that which is genuine and enduring. We must dedicate our time and our talents to the task of edifying the church and gathering souls for the kingdom of God.

CHAPTER SIX

CULTURE

When Nelson Mandela was inaugurated as President of South Africa, it was exciting and very interesting to watch the jubilation of the platform participants and attendees as they sang and danced during the ceremony. By contrast, when William Jefferson Clinton was inaugurated as President of the United States it was a very solemn ceremony, although a joyous occasion. The music was very stately and the program participants were somewhat somber in demeanor. Two presidential inaugurations and yet the behavioral response of each event was so very different. Was one response indeed more appropriate than the other? The answer is no. Each response was appropriate according to the culture in which the events took place. Before proceeding, it should be understood that this discussion refers to people groups around the world and not the myriad subcultures within each society.

Simply put, *culture* is nothing more than the characteristic features and behavior of a group of people and the ideas and values that they espouse. "It is the sum total of their language, dialect, thoughts, actions, and behavior that has been learned and transmitted through the years" (Titon: 1-9). It becomes their badge of identity. A knowledge and understanding of cultural differences helps to increase one's level of tolerance, acceptance, and appreciation, for now, that which was once unfamiliar can be understood on its own terms—as the people understand it.

In terms of music, each culture has its own belief system and ideas as to what it is. This involves value judgments about *aesthetics* (judgments of what is proper and beautiful); *contexts* (when performed, how often, the occasion, its associated lifestyles, etc.); its social organization (age, gender, race, ethnic, work groups); its *status of musicians* (trained or not); *style elements* (recognizable sounds of pitch, meter, timbre, dynamics, etc. that a group understands as its own); *genres* (standard units of repertory); text (a mixture of language and music); *composition* (individual or by group); its *transmission* (a system of notation, oral, imitation, memory); and *movement* (physical activity; playing an instrument to produce sound, dance). Other aspects involve the tangible things that can be seen, felt, used—things that a culture produces. "Its tools and technology give information about the history and way of life while value judgments are based upon criteria from inside a culture, not the imposed external standards that a group does not recognize" (Titon: 1-9).

For example, the term "black music" is more or less a label that has been attached to a *style* and sonority of music (and the liturgy) that is generally associated with African American culture because it bears certain ethnic characteristics that express the experience of this group of people; i.e. compound meter (sometimes referred to as long meter), rich harmonies, rhythm, syncopation, improvisation, bending and surging of notes, ornamentation, blues notes, etc.

In terms of *church music*, there appears to be two schools of thought, the *conservative style* and the *liberal style*, both of which incorporate these ethnic characteristics. The conservative style church music is derived from the European tradition because it consists of hymns, anthems, classics, and perhaps some contemporary Christian music. The organ and piano are the main instruments used, although other instruments may be included. This is not to say that the music is dead or dry. On the contrary, some of the most lively, beautiful, and moving music is rendered within this context. It is most interesting to note that the musicians (and pastors), having had some training in music or a great deal of exposure to this style of music, are able to both read music as well as perform by ear.

The liberal style of music, on the other hand, is more Pentecostal and improvisational in nature, and usually consists of gospel music that fosters a foot-tapping, hand-clapping, and body-swaying response. Nowadays instrumentation includes drums, electric guitars, and synthesizers which are coupled with the piano and organ. In most cases, the musicians (and pastors), although quite talented, have had little or no training, and as a result, perform mainly *by ear*. Because music within this context is erroneously called, by some, *"heritage"* music, the quest for cultural preservation is at times taken to the extreme. Parenthetically speaking, it is interesting to note that churches of all denominations now have both types of worship.

By definition, "heritage" music is that which has been passed on to succeeding generations. Unfortunately for some, heritage music is considered to be that which is currently produced by today's African American musicians—Kirk Franklin and the Family, Yolanda Adams, Vanessa Mitchell, Edwin Hawkins, Andre Crouch, etc. The *contemporary style* of these musicians is really a fusion of today's popular sounds. Black heritage music really begins with the spiritual. It is most unfortunate that these songs are not sung very often. Notwithstanding the myriad reasons for why this is the case, the circumstances under which these songs were born are a tragic reminder of the cruelty and degradation that our ancestors suffered, and even in today's society "the more things change, the more they stay the same." Whatever the reason, many from this ethnic group, still victims of social injustice and economic slavery, tend to gravitate toward and claim that which is current as its "heritage" music. Although looking back can be painful, we must look back "lest our feet stray from the places, our God, where we met Thee; lest our hearts, drunk with the wine of the world, we forget Thee" (Johnson).

When God confused the languages at the tower of Babel and subsequently *"scattered [the people] abroad from thence upon the face of all the earth,"* this was the beginning of cultural diversity, each people group being relevant in its own uniqueness. Parenthetically speaking, although human beings became physically separated, they were, in essence, still members of one family—the family of God. It is for this reason that God expects us to love one another and treat one another with kindness and respect.

In light of this, one could certainly ask whether or not *culture* really matters with God, especially when it comes to worship. Is there one particular cultural standard that God expects for us to adhere to? Are the value judgments that we tend to interpret as being *God's ideal* for worship really His? Being a God of variety, He understands that all forms of worship are shaped by culture and environment. That is His *gift of uniqueness* to humanity. And today He is indeed worshiped in a variety of ways according to culture, style, and geographic location, even within the same denomination. With such diversity, it is no wonder that there is confusion as to what is *right* and *acceptable* worship. " No distinction on account of nationality, race, or caste, is recognized by God. He is the maker of all mankind. All men are of one family by creation, and all are one through redemption. Christ came to demolish every wall of partition; to throw open every compartment of the temple, that every soul may have free access to God" (White: COL 386).

Catholicism, the predominant religion in Europe, has influenced many other religions and cultures throughout the world. It is most interesting to note that those who practice Catholicism have one universal standard of worship despite race, culture, size, status, or geographic location. Why is this not the case within the Seventh-day Adventist Church? Although we do not espouse that belief system, our liturgy contains some of the very same elements—introits, hymns, prayers, responses, communion, etc. What is so *European* about those elements? Which, if any, should be deleted from our ritual? Is worship in the *European tradition* really the standard by which we are to worship God? Could the discussion in the "Introduction" on the *"new world order"* be connected to this issue? When concern over such issues distracts us from focusing our attention upon God, you can be sure that the enemy has successfully planted his seeds of discord so that he can divide and conquer, and in the end, lead his captives to perdition. As a reminder **GOD SAYS...**

Matthew 13:24-28

"The kingdom of heaven is likened unto a man which soweth good seed in his field: But while men slept, his enemy came and sowed tares among the wheat, and went his way. But when the blade was sprung up, and brought forth fruit, then appeared the tares also. So the servants of the householder came and said unto him, Sir, didst not thou sow good seed in thy field? from whence then hath it tares? He said unto them, An enemy hath done this...."

1 Peter 5:8

"Be sober, be vigilant; because your adver-

*sary the devil, as a roaring lion, walketh
about, seeking whom he may devour."*

After pondering these and other questions for a while and praying
for light on the subject, God impressed me with the idea that the cause of
the problem may not necessarily be with the liturgy itself but with the
musical "language" and "dialect" that is used.

"Language is a communication tool made up of a vocabulary that is
understandable and *meaningful* to the hearer." The "dialect" associated
with the language is what groups people together and becomes their
identification badge of kinship. Anyone who speaks the language with a
different dialect is usually called a "foreigner." When Paul listed
"tongues"as one of the spiritual gifts I believe this meant not only the
ability to speak different languages but the dialects as well. Those persons who possess this gift are indeed blessed because they are spared
from the frustration of not being able to communicate, especially when
an interpreter is not available. This brings to mind one of my experiences
while traveling in Europe.

The Trans-European Division of the Seventh-day Adventist Church
invited me to conduct a music seminar for its Youth Congress in
Budapest, Hungary. I had no problem communicating with the youth
from the different countries because they could either speak or understand English, or an interpreter was provided. This was especially necessary for the Hungarians because their language has no resemblance to the
Germanic languages. After the seminar I had planned to spend a couple
of weeks sightseeing around Europe and did not want to be encumbered
with excess baggage, so I went to the post office to ship a box of things
home. When my turn came to be served I told the clerk what I wanted.
However, the look on her face told me that she did not understand a word
I said. In frustration I began to ask those standing in line if anyone could
speak English. Finally a daring soul came forward (only able to speak a
few words of English) and helped me to fill out the form to mail my pack-
age. This situation illumined my understanding of what Paul meant when
he said *"Therefore if I know not the meaning of the voice, I shall be unto him
that speaketh a barbarian, and he that speaketh shall be a barbarian unto me" (1
Corinthians 14:11).* This is exactly how I felt that day.

There are other kinds of languages that exist. For example, there is legal language, street language, professional language, sports language, academic language, musical language, and the list goes on. To further illustrate the point, if the vocabulary of any of the above is configured in a way that all cannot understand, then it becomes a "foreign language" and is utterly useless to the hearer. The same is true for music, and as is the case with the English language, "musical ebonics," which I believe is an underlying cause of the controversy, has crept into the church and has changed the "language" and "dialect" from sacred to commercial sounding music.

When African slaves were brought to America, they were stripped of two very important elements of any culture—music and language— and were forced to speak and sing in a vernacular that was totally foreign to them. As time passed, however, they developed a vocabulary and dialect that became distinctly their own. Hence, a new culture was born. Resistence to, and rejection of the *European* tradition of music comes then when it is imposed upon this culture and is elevated as "the standard" because it serves as a reminder of this unfortunate situation. The psychological scars have not yet healed, and as a result, this conflict has affected the worship experience of many. "Walls of separation have been built up between the whites and the blacks. These walls of prejudice will tumble down of themselves as did the walls of Jericho, when Christians obey the Word of God, which enjoins on them supreme love to their Maker and impartial love to their neighbors" (White: SW 43).

In worship the operative word is *edification*. If the *"language"* is foreign to the congregation it is irrelevant and meaningless and becomes as *"sounding brass, or a tinkling cymbal."* This calls to mind another experience to illustrate this point. I attended church in France where the entire service was conducted in French—without an interpreter. Although I went to worship God, I was not really edified because I could not understand or relate to anything, not even the hymns. I could not even interact socially because of the language barrier. The same seems to be true for music. When music is rendered in a "language" and dialect that is foreign to the hearer, it is meaningless. The message is lost, and the church is not edified. This is one reason why the Catholic church finally permitted the Mass to be conducted in the vernacular of the people. If the musical language is foreign to the congregation, how can it be edified? "When human beings [render music] with the Spirit and the understanding, heavenly musicians take up the strain, and join in the song of thanksgiving. He who has bestowed upon us all the gifts that enable us to be workers together with God, expects His servants to cultivate their voices, so that they can speak and sing in a way that all can understand" (White: 9T 143). **GOD SAYS. . .**

1 Corinthians 14:1-5; 6-10,12, 19, 33

"Follow after charity, and desire spiritual gifts, but rather that ye may prophesy. For he that speaketh in an unknown tongue speaketh not unto men but unto God: for no man understandeth him; howbeit in the spirit he speaketh mysteries. But he that prophesieth speaketh unto men to edification, and exhortation, and comfort. He that speaketh in an unknown tongue edifieth himself; but he that prophesieth edifieth the church . . . Now, brethren, if I come unto you speaking with tongues, what shall I profit you, except I shall speak to you either by revelation, or by knowledge, or by prophesying, or by doctrine? And even things without life giving sound, whether pipe or harp, except they give a distinction in the sounds, how shall it be known what is piped or harped? For if the trumpet give an uncertain sound, who shall prepare himself to the battle? So likewise ye, except ye utter by the tongue words easy to be understood, how shall it be known what is spoken? for ye shall speak into the air. There are, it may be, many kinds of voices in the world, and none of them is without signification. . . Even so ye, forasmuch as ye are zealous of spiritual gifts, seek that ye may excel to the edifying of the church. . . Yet in the church I had rather speak five words with my understanding, that by my voice I might teach others also, than ten thousand words in an unknown tongue. . . For God is

*not the author of confusion, but of peace, as
in all churches of the saints."*

The point that I am trying to make is that music in worship must be edifying to the congregation. This is not to say, however, that any and everything is appropriate simply because it is expressed in the vernacular of the culture. On the contrary, this seems to be the case, and in an attempt to *identify* oneself, attention is drawn away from God who is supposed to be the object of our worship. Pre-civil rights movement ministers preached *doctrines* of the church. However, many of the post-civil rights ministers were caught up in culturalism and began to preach the attributes of a race instead of those of Christianity. Thus, the "black power", "black awareness" era was born, and culture was placed in competition with Christianity. The music began to reflect this philosophy as well. We must be cognizant of the miasmatic influence of ethnocentrism that the enemy is using to divert our attention from God. We have been given Christian principles that transcend the boundaries of culture. Because the blood of Jesus Christ was shed for every person in every race, in every culture, what merit do these issues have in light of our salvation? **GOD SAYS...**

Isaiah 56:7, 8

"For my house shall be called an house of prayer for all people. The Lord GOD which gathereth the outcasts of Israel saith, Yet will I gather others to him, besides those that are gathered unto him."

Mark 3:25

"And if a house be divided against itself, that house cannot stand."

John 10:16

"And other sheep I have, which are not of this fold: them also I must bring, and they shall hear my voice; and there shall be one fold, and one shepherd."

John 17: 22, 23

"And the glory which thou gavest me I have given them; that they may be one, even as

we are one. I in them, and thou in me, that they may be perfect in one . . . ."

Act 15:9

"And put no difference between us and them, purifying their hearts by faith."

Romans 3:22

"Even the righteousness of God which is by faith of Jesus Christ unto all and upon all them that believe: for there is no difference."

Romans 6:5

"For if we have been planted together in the likeness of his death, we shall be also in the likeness of his resurrection."

1 Corinthians 7:19

"Circumcision is nothing, and uncircumcision is nothing, but the keeping of the commandments of God."

I Corinthians 12:13

"For by one Spirit are we all baptized into one body, whether we be Jews or Gentiles, whether we be bond or free; and have been all made to drink into one Spirit."

Galatians 3:28

"There is neither Jew nor Greek, there is neither bond nor free, there is neither male nor female: for ye are all one in Christ Jesus."

Galatians 5:6

"For in Jesus Christ neither circumcision availeth anything, nor uncircumcision; but faith which worketh by love."

Ephesians 2:14

"For he is our peace, who hath made both one, and hath broken down the middle wall of partition between us."

Ephesians 4:4-6

"There is one body, and one Spirit, even as ye are called in one hope of your calling;

> *One Lord, one faith, one baptism, One God*
> *and Father of all. . . and in you all. "*

"Thus Christ sought to teach the disciples the truth that in God's kingdom there are no territorial lines. No caste, no aristocracy; that they must go to all nations, bearing to them the message of a Saviour's love" (White: AA 20).

Summary

Culture is the badge of identity of people groups that characterizes its music, language, dialect, behavior, ideas, and values, and is learned and transmitted from one generation to the next. It is the *gift of uniqueness* that God has given to humanity.

In worship God must be glorified and the church edified; culture is purely incidental. However, when culture becomes the issue, the focus, and the foundation upon which worship is based, problems of attitudes, beliefs, and practices begin to surface, for it is at this point that the true motive for worship is lost in the ritual. "The religion of the Bible recognizes no caste or color. It ignores rank wealth, worldly honor. God estimates men as men. With Him, character decides their worth. And we are to recognize the Spirit of Christ in whomsoever he is revealed" (White: 9T 223).

When Jesus returns He is coming to redeem people from all nations, kindreds, tongues, and peoples. In preparation for this glorious event, we must learn to tolerate, accept, and appreciate cultural diversity for what it is. We must tear down the walls of prejudice that so often create separation and division among the people in God's beautiful rainbow of colors. "The walls of sectarianism and caste and race will fall down when the true missionary spirit enters the hearts of men. Prejudice is melted away by the love of God" (White: SW 55).

"When the Holy Spirit is poured out, there will be a triumph of humanity over prejudice in seeking the salvation of the souls of human beings. God will control minds. Human hearts will love as Christ loved. And the color line will be regarded by many very differently from the way in which it is now regarded. To love as Christ loves lifts the mind into a pure, heavenly, unselfish atmosphere" (White: 9T 209).

CHAPTER SEVEN

WORSHIP

Human beings were created with an innate need to worship some one or some thing. The Bible tells us that during ancient times those who did not know or believe in the God of Creation made and worshiped gods of wood and stone according to the attributes of their own imaginations. There were even those who worshiped the sun, moon, and stars. Even today the god of materialism, and even oneself are the objects of worship for many. "The duty to worship God is based upon the fact that He is the Creator, and that to Him all other beings owe their existence. And whenever in the Bible His claim to reverence and worship above the gods of the heathen is presented, there is cited the evidence of His creative power" (White: GC 436).

God not only wants us to worship Him, but He also wants possession of our hearts and minds by choice, not by coercion or deception. "The exercise of force is contrary to the principles of God's government; He desires only the service of love; and love cannot be commanded; it cannot be won by force or authority. Only by love is love awakened. To know God is to love Him; His character must by manifested in contrast to the character of Satan" (White: DA 2).

In contemplating the theme of worship, a phrase from the Lord's prayer came to mind—*"Thy will be done in earth, as is in heaven"* (Matthew 6:10). God has pulled back the curtain, through visions given to his prophets, to give us a peak at worship in the heavenly kingdom. This is what they saw:

Isaiah 6:1-4

"In the year that King Uzziah died I saw also the Lord sitting upon a throne, high and lifted up, and His train filled the temple. Above it stood the seraphims: each one had six wings; with twain he covered his face, and with twain he covered his feet, and with twain he did fly. And one cried unto another, and said Holy, holy, holy is the LORD of hosts: the whole earth is full of His glory. And the posts of the door moved at the voice of Him that cried, and the house was filled with smoke."

Revelation 4:2-4, 6, 8, 10, 11

"And immediately I was in the spirit: and, behold, a throne was set in heaven, and one sat on the throne. . . And round about the throne were four and twenty seats: and upon the seats I saw four and twenty elders sitting, clothed in white raiment; and they had on their heads crowns of gold. . . And round about the throne, were four beasts. . . And they rest not day and night, saying, Holy, holy, holy, Lord God Almighty, which was, and is, and is to come. . . The four and twenty elders. . . cast their crowns before the throne, saying, Thou art worthy, O Lord, to receive glory and honour and power . . . ."

From these two scenes, it is clear that in heaven, endless praise is rendered unto God day and night. He is indeed the focal point of all worship, and it is His desire that the same expressions of adoration and praise be rendered unto Him on earth in remembrance of His love, mercy, forgiveness, longsuffering, goodness, kindness, blessings, protection, salvation, and faithfulness toward us. Such worship results in attitudes and behaviors that engender reverence and humility, and bear witness to our having had a meaningful encounter with Him.

Today there are numerous denominations and styles of worship—Anglicans, Baptists, Catholics, Episcopals, Jehovah's Witnesses, Lutherans, Methodists, Pentecostals, Presbyterians, Seventh-day Adventists, to name a few, and to further complicate things, the style of worship of some of these churches can differ depending upon size, culture, and geographic location. Lest we forget, there are also the snake handlers and other sects that should be added to the list. With such a variety to choose from, it is no wonder that one could become confused as to what worship is, how it should be done, where it should be done, when it should be done, who does it, what happens when it is done; in other words, what is the *"right"* and *"acceptable way"* to worship God.

"Unless correct ideas of true worship and true reverence are impressed upon the people, there will be a growing tendency to place the sacred and the eternal on a level with common things, and those professing the truth will be an offense to God and a disgrace to religion" (White: 5T 500).

The key to beginning to understand this issue of worship is rooted in Genesis 1:1, 31: *"In the beginning God created the heaven and the earth. And God saw every thing that He had made, and, behold, it was very good. . . ."* Simply put, God, the Creator, deserves to be worshiped by His creatures. There is nothing more beautiful or breath-taking than to drive through a wooded area on a bright, sunny autumn day when the tree leaves are at their peak of brilliant color. Consider the many species of birds, plants, flowers, trees, animals, and creeping things. Each in its own way, according to its own order, renders a testimony of praise to the Creator. Even to the inanimate objects of creation, **GOD SAYS. . .**

Psalm 19:1-4

"THE HEAVENS declare the glory of God; and the firmament showeth his handiwork. Day unto day uttereth speech, and night unto night showeth knowledge. There is no speech nor language, where their voice is not heard. Their line is gone out through all the earth, and their words to the end of the world. In them hath He set a tabernacle for the sun."

Psalm 65:13

"The pastures are clothed with flocks; the valleys also are covered over with corn; they shout for joy, they also sing."

Psalm 96:11, 12

"Let the heavens rejoice, and let the earth be glad; let the sea roar, and the fullness there of. Let the field be joyful, and all that is therein: then shall all the trees of the wood rejoice."

Psalm 97:1-6

"The LORD reigneth; let the earth rejoice; let the multitude of isles be glad thereof. Clouds and darkness are round about him. . . A fire goeth before him, and burneth up his enemies round about. His lightnings enlighten the world: the earth saw, and trembled. The hills melted like wax at the presence of the Lord, at the presence of the LORD of the whole earth. The heavens declare His righteousness. . . . ."

Psalm 98:7-9

"Let the sea roar, and the fulness thereof; the world and they that dwell therein. Let the floods clap their hands: let the hills be joyful together Before the LORD . . . ."

Psalm 148:3-10

"Praise ye him, sun and moon: praise him, all ye stars of light. Praise him, ye heavens of heavens, and ye waters that be above the heavens. Let them praise the name of the LORD: for he commanded, and they were created. He hath also stablished them forever and ever: he hath made a decree which shall not pass. Praise the Lord from the earth, ye dragons, and all deeps: Fire, and hail; snow, and vapours; stormy wind fulfilling His word: Mountains, and all hills; fruitful trees and all cedars: Beasts, and all *cattle; creeping things, and flying fowl.*"

"The beauties of nature have a tongue that speaks to us without ceasing. The open heart can be impressed with the love and glory of God as seen in the works of His hand. The listening ear can hear and understand the communications of God through the things of nature. There is a lesson in the sunbeam and in the various objects of nature that God has presented to our view. The green fields, the lofty trees, the buds and flowers, the passing cloud, the falling rain, the babbling brook, the sun, moon, and stars in the heavens—all invite our attention and meditation, and bid us become acquainted with Him which make them all" (White: TMK 144).

As a noun, worship is simply a religious practice of beliefs and rituals (order of service, holy communion, baptism, the trinity, stewardship, the Sabbath, the state of the dead, etc.). As a verb, worship is the expression of praise, adoration, and devotion to a divine being or supernatural power that possesses one's affections. Since worship is the primary issue over which the battle between good and evil continues to be fought, **GOD SAYS...**

Isaiah 42:8	"*I am the LORD: that is my name: and my glory will I not give to another, neither my praise to graven images.*"
John 4:24	"*God is a Spirit: and they that worship him must worship him in spirit and in truth.*"
2 Thessalonians 2:15	"*Stand fast, and hold the traditions which we have been taught, whether by word, or our epistle.*"
1 John 1:6, 7	"*If we say that we have fellowship with him, and walk in darkness, we lie, and do not the truth: but if we walk in the light, as he is in the*"

— 44 —

*light, we have fellowship one with another,
and the blood of Jesus Christ his Son
cleanseth us from all sin."*

Revelation 14:7,9,10   *"Fear God and give glory to him. . . . And
worship him that made heaven and earth. If
any man worship the beast and his image. . .
the same shall drink of the wine of the wrath
of God. . . ."*

There are three contexts in which worship takes place—the "secret closet" (individual), the small group, and the congregation. Each one, though different in nature and function, is necessary, and impacts upon one's spiritual growth and development.

The motivation to *worship* God is generated by love. True worship comes from the heart, and from having a *personal encounter* with Him seven days a week, not just on the designated day of assembly. That which we feed and nurture will flourish and grow. The more time we spend with God the deeper our love and appreciation for Him will be. "Religion is not to be confined to external forms and ceremonies. The religion that comes from God is the only religion that will lead to God. In order to serve Him aright, we must be born of the divine Spirit. This will purify the heart and renew the mind, giving us a new capacity for knowing and loving God. It will give us a willing obedience to all His requirements. This is true worship. It is the fruit of the working of the Holy Spirit" (White: DA 95).

In order to accomplish this one must have the "secret closet" experience. This is the time in which we can have audience with God in a private, intimate setting, where we can express our gratitude for His blessings and lay bare our souls, confessing faults and sins, making our requests known, praying intercessory prayers for others, seeking guidance, and praying about things that dare not be spoken to another human being. It is also a time in which we can laugh with God, for He does indeed have a sense of humor. To this form of worship **GOD SAYS. . .**

2 Chronicles 7:14,15   *"If my people, which are called by my name,
shall humble themselves, and pray, and seek*

my face, and turn from their wicked ways; then will I hear from heaven, and will forgive their sin, and will heal their land. Now my eyes shall be open, and mine ears attent unto the prayer that is made in this place."

Psalm 55:17

"Evening, and morning, and at noon, will I pray, and cry aloud: and he shall hear my voice."

Proverbs 15:8

"The prayer of the upright is his delight."

Isaiah 1:18

"Come now, and let us reason together, saith the LORD. . ."

Matthew 6:6,7

"But thou, when thou prayest, enter into thy closet, and when thou hast shut thy door, pray to thy Father which is in secret; and thy Father which seeth in secret shall reward thee openly. But when ye pray, use not vain repetitions. . . For your Father knoweth what things ye have need of, before ye ask him."

Matthew 21:22

"And all things, whatsoever ye ask in prayer, believing, ye shall receive."

Luke 18:1

"Men ought always to pray, and not to faint."

1 Corinthians 14:15

"I will pray with the spirit, and I will pray with the understanding also. . . ."

Ephesians 6:18

"Praying always with all prayer and supplication in the Spirit, and watching thereunto with all perseverance and supplication for all saints."

Philippians 4:6

"Be careful for nothing; but in every thing by prayer and supplication with thanksgiving let your requests be made known unto God. And the peace of God, which passeth all understanding, shall keep your hearts and minds through Christ Jesus."

1 Thessalonians 5:17

"Pray without ceasing."

Hebrews 4:16

"Let us therefore come boldly unto the throne of grace, that we may obtain mercy, and find grace to help in time of need."

James 5:16

"The effectual fervent prayer of a righteous man availeth much."

"Prayer is the opening of the heart to God as to a friend. Not that it is necessary in order to make known to God what we are, but in order to enable us to receive him. Prayer does not bring God down to us, but brings us up to him" (White: SC 63).

When one emerges from such an encounter with God, not only will there be praise, thanksgiving, and rejoicing, but as outlined in Isaiah 6:1-13, several other things shall have happened as well. First of all, this type of worship makes us aware of God's presence—He is the focus of attention. Second, it makes us aware of our own sinful state while, at the same time, it provides us with an opportunity to confess our sins, believing that He has forgiven us as promised in 1 John 1:9. Third, we have an opportunity to renew our commitment to serve Him. Finally, we have an opportunity to demonstrate our love for Him by accepting the commission to go and witness to others. Thus we worship Him in spirit (with the right attitude) and in truth (intelligently).

Worship such as this is not preoccupied with liturgy or anything else that would distract from this two-way communication with God. In my *"secret closet"* I, too, have experienced interacting with God, and can truly say that there is nothing like that warm, close feeling that comes from such an encounter. The Bible gives us examples of the different types of encounters with God that other individuals had:

Genesis 5:24

"And Enoch walked with God: and he was not; for God took him."

Genesis 32:24, 26, 28

"And Jacob. . . wrestled a man with him until the breaking of the day. . . And he said, Let me go, for the day breaketh. And he [Jacob] said, I will not let thee go, except thou bless me. . . And He said, Thy name shall be called no more Jacob, but Israel: for as a prince hast thou power with God and with men, and hast prevailed."

Exodus 3:4, 6

"God called unto him out of the midst of the bush, and said, Moses, Moses. . . And Moses hid his face; for he was afraid to look upon God."

Leviticus 9:23, 24

"And the glory of the LORD appeared unto all the people. And there came a fire out from before the LORD and consumed upon the altar the burnt offering and the fat, which, when all the people saw, they shouted and fell on their faces."

1 Samuel 5:2, 3

"When the Philistines took the ark of God, they brought it into the house of Dagon, and set it by Dagon. . . behold, Dagon was fallen upon his face to the earth before the ark of the LORD."

1 Kings 18:36, 38, 39

"And it came to pass at the time of the offering of the evening sacrifice, that Elijah the prophet came near, and said, LORD God of Abraham, Isaac, and of Israel, let it be known this day that thou art God in Israel. . . Then the fire of the LORD fell, and consumed the burnt sacrifice. . . And when all the people saw it, they fell on their faces. . . ."

2 Chronicles 6:1-3; 7:1-3	*"Then said Solomon, . . . I have built an house of habitation for thee, and a place for thy dwelling forever. . . And the glory of the Lord filled the house. And the priest could not enter into the house of the Lord, because the glory of the Lord had filled the Lord's house. And when all the children of Israel saw how the fire came down, and the glory of the Lord upon the house, they bowed themselves with their faces to the ground upon the pavement, and worshiped, and praised the Lord saying, for his mercy endureth forever."*
Job 38:1,4; 40:3,4	*"Then the Lord answered Job out of the whirlwind, and said. . . Where wast thou when I laid the foundations of the earth? Declare, if thou hast understanding. . . Then Job answered the Lord, and said, Behold I am vile; what shall I answer thee? I will lay my hand upon my mouth."*
Isaiah 38:1-5	*"In those days was Hezekiah sick unto death . . . And Isaiah, the prophet. . . said unto him Thus saith the Lord, set thine house in order: for thou shalt die, and not live. . . Then Hezekian turned his face toward the wall, and prayed unto the Lord, and said, remember now, O Lord, I beseech thee, how I have walked before Thee in truth and with a perfect heart, and have done that which is good in thy sight. . . Then came the word of the Lord. . . I have heard thy prayer, I have seen thy tears: behold, I will add unto thy days fifteen years."*
Luke 6: 12	*"And it came to pass in those days, that he [Jesus] went out into a mountain to pray,*

and continued all night in prayer to God."

Unfortunately, when individual worship is neglected, whether due to time restraints or other challenges, one is unarmed and unprepared to fight off the enemy and the custom-made temptations with which he seeks to ensnare the unsuspecting soul. "Do not neglect secret prayer, for it is the soul of religion" (White: 1T 163).

The second context for worship is that of the small group—family worship, Bible study groups, etc. Even in this context one can have a personal encounter with God through the sharing of personal testimonies, encouraging one another, and exchanging ideas. Family worship is not only the glue that bonds families together, but it is also one of the most important means of involving the children in worship. For them it can and should be the time in which principles and moral values are instilled. The memory of family worship in my home, especially on Friday evenings, is something that I will never forget, for it was in this setting that I had my first encounter with God at age five. I felt the Holy Spirit moving upon my heart, and at that moment I wanted to surrender my life to Him.

In worship we sang all of the hymns pertaining to the Sabbath and other songs, and were given the opportunity to choose our favorite scripture reading. My youngest sister used to enjoy reading "the minutes" from worship the previous week (something she learned to do from what was practiced in Sabbath School in those days), and after worship, we could look forward to a scrumptious meal that my mother would have prepared.

Our children and our youth need to be rooted and nurtured in our religious beliefs and moral values in order to be able to face the challenges of life in today's world. It is important for the children to be able to have a forum in which they can have an active part; otherwise, the enemy will capture their souls. In order to avoid this, **GOD SAYS. . .**

Deuteronomy 6:6-9

"And these words, which I command thee this day, shall be in thine heart: and thou shalt teach them diligently unto thy children, and shalt talk of them when thou sittest in thine house, and when thou walkest by the

way, and when thou liest down, and when thou risest up. And thou shalt bind them for a sign upon thine hand, and they shall be as frontlets between thine eyes. And thou shalt write them upon the posts of thy house, and on thy gates."

Proverbs 22:6

"Train up a child in the way he should go: and when he is old, he will not depart from it."

Isaiah 54:13

"And all thy children shall be taught of the LORD; and great shall be the peace of thy children."

"In every Christian home God should be honored by the morning and evening sacrifices of prayer and praise. . . It is the duty of Christian parents, morning and evening, by earnest prayer and persevering faith, to make a hedge about their children" (White: CPT 110).

The third and more complex context in which worship occurs is the congregation. The expression, "going to church", is often used to describe this experience. Ideally, this should represent the culmination of all of the worship experiences that occurred during the week.

"To the humble, believing soul, the house of God on earth is the gate of heaven. The song of praise, the prayer, the words spoken by Christ's representatives, are God's appointed agencies to prepare a people for the church above, for that loftier worship into which there can enter nothing that defileth. . . Nothing that is sacred, nothing that pertains to the worship of God, should be treated with carelessness or indifference" (White: 5T 491).

The word "church" has several different connotations. Isaiah referred to it as *"an house of prayer."* Jesus referred to it as His *"bride,"* the object of His love and affection, the *"woman"* for whom He will come the second time. Paul referred to it as a *"body."* However, "church" and "worship" are quite different in theory and practice. I once read a little thought printed in our bulletin that said "There is no **CH—RCH** without 'U'." How true that statement is. Human beings are social creatures;

therefore we are admonished to attend church in order to exhort and encourage one another, and help build up the body of Christ. **GOD SAYS...**

1 Corinthians 12:25,26	*"The members should have the same care for one another. And whether one member suffer, all the members suffer with it; or one member be honoured, all the members rejoice with it."*
1 Corinthians 14:26	*"Let all things be done unto edifying."*
Ephesians 5:19	*"Speaking to yourselves in psalms and hymns and spiritual songs, singing and making melody in your heart to the Lord."*
Hebrews 10:25	*"Not forsaking the assembling of ourselves together. . . but exhorting one another . . . ."*

From personal observation, each congregation seems to have its own personality and temperament just like humans—sanguine, choleric, melancholy, and phlegmatic. This is why members, like birds of a feather flocking together, may feel more comfortable in one church setting as opposed to another. They gravitate toward the church that best *edifies* them—where they can relate to the *"language"* and the *"dialect."* This also includes academic environments wherein the musical "language and dialect" is different from non-academic settings. Negative attitudes and unfair, erroneous value judgments are often directed toward those who speak and understand this "language" simply because it is different from the cultural vernacular.

Although the church is a "body" of believers that assemble to collectively worship, study, hear the spoken Word, and enjoy the fellowship of one another, "service" is one of its main purposes and function. This is the reason for organizing community service centers, establishing jail and nursing home bands, inreach and outreach ministries, and other church programs. One can only imagine what the life span of a church would be without these programs. The members would eventually stop coming and the church would die. The words of the Negro spiritual, *"Ain't Got Time To Die,"* correctly summarize the true meaning of what worship and praise are really all about— *"When I'm feeding the poor, I'm praising my Jesus. . . . when I'm healing the sick, I'm praising my Jesus. . . , when I'm giving my all, I'm praising my Jesus. . . ."* From this, one should be able to see that praise to God involves much more than an outburst of joy or high-spirited music during a worship service. **GOD SAYS. . .**

Isaiah 58:6-8

"Is not this the fast that I have chosen? to loose the bands of wickedness, to undo the heavy burdens, and to let the oppressed go free, and that ye break every yoke? Is it not to deal thy bread to the hungry, and that thou bring the poor that are cast out to thy house? when thou seest the naked, that thou cover him; and that thou hide not thy self from thine own flesh? Then shall thy light break forth as the morning, and thine health shall spring forth speedily: and thy righteousness shall go forth before thee; the glory of the Lord shall be thy rereward."

Matthew 20:26-28

"But whosoever will be great among you, let him be your minister; And whosoever will be chief among you, let him be your servant: Even as the Son of man came not to be ministered unto, but to minister, and to give his life a ransom for many."

Matthew 28:19,20

"Go ye therefore, and teach all nations, baptizing them in the name of the Father, and of the Son, and of the Holy Ghost: Teaching them to observe all things whatsoever I have commanded you: and lo, I am with you always, even unto the end of the world."

Hebrews 10:24

"And let us consider one another to provoke

unto love and to good works."

1 John 3:18   *"My little children, let us not love in word, neither in tongue; but in deed and in truth."*

The church is also an *"organization."* Unlike individual and small group worship, the dynamics involved necessitate establishing rules and guidelines (a church manual) that the members agree to abide by in order to avoid confusion and chaos. Since law and order are the rule of heaven, **GOD SAYS. . .**

Romans 12:4, 5   *"For as we have many members in one body, and all members have not the same office: So we, being many, are one body in Christ, and every one members one of another."*

Romans 13:1-7   *"LET EVERY soul be subject unto the higher powers. For there is no power but of God. Whosoever therefore resisteth the power, resisteth the ordinance of God . . For rulers are not a terror to good works, but to the evil. . . For he is the minister of God, a revenger to execute wrath upon him that doeth evil . . . Wherefore ye must needs be subject, not only for wrath, but also for conscience sake. For this cause pay tribute also: for they are God's ministers, attending continually upon this very thing."*

1 Corinthians 12:4-26   *"Now there are diversities of gifts, but the same Spirit. And there are differences of administrations, but the same Lord. And there are diversities of operations, but it is the same God which worketh all in all. But the manifestation of the Spirit is given to every man to profit withal . . . But all these worketh that one and the selfsame Spirit, dividing to every man severally as He will. . . And those members of the body, which we think to be less honorable, upon these we bestow more abundant honor; and our uncomely parts have more abundant comeliness. . . That there should be no schism in the body; but that the members should have the same care for one another. And whether one member suffer, all the members suffer with it; or one member be honored, all the members rejoice with it."*

1 Corinthians 15:40
"Let all things be done decently and in order."

Ephesians 4:11-15
"And he gave some, apostles; and some, prophets; and some, evangelists,; and some, pastors and teachers; For the perfection of the saints, for the work of the ministry, for the edifying of the body of Christ: Till we all come in the unity of the faith, and of the knowledge of the Son of God, unto a perfect man, unto the measure of the stature of the fullness of Christ. . . Speaking the truth in love, may grow up into him in all things, which is the head, even Christ."

Church organization is nothing new. It can be traced back to Antiquity when God appointed the Levites to run the church (see 1 & 2 Chronicles). Holy Writ even records an instance whereby such organization eliminated the conflict that arose in the early Christian church:

Acts 6:1-8
"AND IN those days, when the number of the disciples was multiplied, there arose a murmuring of the Grecians against the Hebrews, because their widows were neglected in the daily ministration. Then the twelve called the multitude of the disciples

unto them, and said, it is not reason that we should leave the word of God, and serve tables. Wherefore, brethren, look ye out among you seven men of honest report, full of the Holy Ghost and wisdom, whom we may appoint over this business. But we will give ourselves continually to prayer, and to the ministry of the word. And the saying pleased the whole multitude: and they chose Stephen, a man full of faith and of the Holy Ghost, and Philip and Prochorus, and Nicanor, and Timon, and Parmenas, and Nicolas as a proselyte of Antioch: whom they set before the apostles: and when they had prayed, they laid their hands on them. And the word of God increased; and the number of the disiples multiplied in Jerusalem greatly; and a great company of the priests were obedient to the faith. And Stephen, full of faith and power, did great wonders and miracles among the people."

Unfortunately, as with all organizations, the cancer of *politics* has proven to be one of the greatest diseases of the church, and one of the greatest hindrances to worship. Instead of acting upon principle, decisions are often made according to "who you know," or upon one's education, wealth, and pedigree. From the President down to the deacon, nominating persons to serve in the various capacities of the church is one of the most politically sensitive times. Of course, church politics is nothing new. Miriam criticized Moses for listening to Zipporah, his wife, instead of consulting with her; the mother of James and John sought a high position for her sons next to Jesus; and it was politics that motivated the Scribes and Pharisees to kill Jesus Christ.

"Honesty and policy will not work together in the same mind. In time, either policy will be expelled, and truth and honesty reign supreme, or, if policy is cherished, honesty will be forgotten. They are never in agreement; they have nothing in common. One is the prophet of

Baal,;the other is the true prophet of God" (White: 5T 96).

Another part of the organizational structure of the church is the *ritual*, a symbolic reminder of one's beliefs (worship, baptism, communion, etc.). It provides structure and order and can be implemented in a variety of ways. One of the deceptions of the enemy is that of leading us to believe that the ritual itself is worship when in fact, it is only a *form* of worship. Such thinking can lead to false worship—worshiping for the wrong reason.

"Not by seeking a holy mountain or a sacred temple are men brought into communion with heaven. Religion is not to be confined to external forms and ceremonies. The religion that comes from God is the only religion that will lead to God. In order to serve Him aright, we must be born of the divine spirit. This will purify the heart and renew the mind, giving us a new capacity for knowing and loving God. It will give us a willing obedience to all His requirements. This is true worship. It is the fruit of the working of the Holy Spirit. By the Spirit every sincere prayer is indited, and such prayer is acceptable to God. Whenever a soul reaches out after God, there the Spirit's working is manifest, and God will reveal Himself to that soul. For such worshippers he is seeking. He waits to receive them, and to make them his sons and daughters" (White: DA 96).

"Everyone should feel that he has a part to act in making the Sabbath meetings interesting. You are not to come together simply as a matter of form, but for the interchange of thought, for the relation of your daily experiences, for the expression of thanksgiving for the utterance of your sincere desire for divine enlightenment, that you may know God, and Jesus Christ, whom he has sent. Communing together in regard to Christ will strengthen the soul for life's trials and conflicts."

"Never think that you can be Christians and yet withdraw yourselves within yourselves. Each one is a part of the great web of humanity, and the experience of his associates. . . We must carry to every religious gathering a quickened spiritual consciousness that God and his angels are there, cooperating with all true worshippers. As you enter the place of worship, ask the Lord to remove all evil from your heart. Bring to His house only that which He can bless. Kneel before God in His temple, and consecrate to Him His own, which He has purchased with the blood of Jesus Christ. . . The place of worship may be very humble, but it is no less acknowledged by God. To those who worship God in spirit and in truth, and the beauty of holiness it will be as the gate of heaven" (White: 6T 362, 363).

In false worship, the motivation for *"going to church"* is preoccupied with external issues, preconceived ideas, and concerns—personal expectations, culture, liturgy, music, etc. Man then becomes the audience, the focus of attention, and the "strange fire" kindled by external stimuli, especially the music, and the craving of an emotional *"high"* is the only thing that seems to satisfy the empty soul. Thus many believe that they are filled with the Holy Spirit when in reality, they are only physically responding to the *sound stimulus* that secretes a hormone that makes them feel that way, especially wherein the music is high-spirited. It is interesting to note that the feelings of euphoria from the reaction to such music are the same as those when one falls in love because the same hormone is secreted. (see Chapter Twelve)

"If we work to create an excitement of feeling, we shall have all we want, and more than we can possibly know how to manage. . . We must not regard it as our work to create an excitement. The Holy Spirit of God alone can create a healthy enthusiasm. Let God work, and let the human agent walk softly before Him, watching, waiting, praying, looking unto Jesus every moment, led and controlled by the precious spirit, which is light and life" (White: 2SM 16).

Artificial stimulants in worship are like empty calories—they satisfy for the moment but provide no nourishment for spiritual growth and development. If genuine heart-felt praise was indeed rendered to God, that "high" that is so often externally obtained would come naturally. Today the buzz words associated with this type of worship are "celebration" or "praise." "It is no real evidence that you are a Christian because your emotion is stirred, your spirit is stirred by truth. The question is, are you growing up into Christ, your living head? Is the grace of Christ manifested in your life?. . . God's grace is ever working upon the human heart, and when it is received, the evidence of its reception will appear in the life and character of its recipient, for spiritual life will be seen developing from within. The grace of Christ in the heart will always promote spiritual life, and spiritual advancement will be made" (White: TMK 163).

The Bible gives us examples of such worship. Note the behavior of the worshippers:

Exodus 32:1-19

"And the people. . . gathered themselves together unto Aaron, and said unto him, Up, make us gods, which shall go before us. . . And Aaron said unto them, Break off the golden earrings, which are in the ears of your wives, of you sons, and of your daughters, and bring them unto me. . . And after he made it a molten calf: and they said, These be thy gods, O Israel, which brought thee up out of the land of Egypt. . . And when Aaron saw it, he built an altar before it . . . and said, Tomorrow is a feast to the LORD... And the LORD said unto Moses, Go, get thee down; for thy people which thou broughtest out of the land of Egypt, have corrupted themselves: they have turned aside quickly out of the way which I commanded them. . . And Moses turned, and went down from the mount. . . And it came to pass, as soon as he saw the calf, and the dancing: and Moses' anger waxed hot. . . ."

1 Kings 18:22-28

"Then said Elijah unto the people . . . Let them therefore give us two bullocks; and let them choose one bullock for themselves, and cut it in pieces, and lay it on wood, and put no fire under. . . And call ye on the name of your gods, and I will call on the name of the LORD: and the God that answereth by fire, let him be God . . . And it came to pass at noon, that Elijah mocked them, and said, Cry aloud: for he is a god; either he is talking, or he is pursuing, or he is on a journey, or peradventure he sleepeth, and must be awaked. And they cried aloud, and cut themselves after their manner with knives and lancets, till the blood gushed out upon them."

Daniel 3:1-7

"Nebuchadnezzar the King made an image of gold. . . he set it up in the plain of Dura, in the province of Babylon. . . And all the rulers of the provinces were gathered together unto the dedication of the image. . . Then an herald cried aloud, To you it is commanded, O people, nations, and languages, That at what time ye hear the sound of the cornet, flute, harp, sackbut, psaltery, dulcimer, and all kinds of musick, ye fall down and worship the golden image that Nebuchadnezzar the king hath set up: And whoso falleth not down and worshipeth shall the same hour be cast into the midst of a burning fiery furnace. Therefore at that time, when all the people heard the sound of the cornet, flute, harp, sackbut, psaltery, and all kinds of music, all the people, the nations, and the languages, fell down and worshipped the golden image that Nebuchadnezzar the king had set up."

"How often in our own day, is the love of pleasure disguised by a 'form of godliness!' A religion that permits men, while observing the rites of worship, to devote themselves to selfish or sensual gratification, is as pleasing to the multitudes now as in the days of Israel. And there are still pliant Aarons, who, while holding positions of authority in the church, will yield to the desires of the unconsecrated, and thus encourage them in sin" (White: PP 317).

"The manner in which the meetings in Indiana have been carried on, with noise and confusion, does not commend them to thoughtful, intelligent minds. There is nothing in these demonstrations which will convince the world that we have the truth. Mere noise and shouting are no evidence of sanctification, or of the descent of the Holy Spirit. Your wild demonstrations create only disgust in the minds of unbelievers. The fewer of such demonstrations there are, the better it will be for the actors and for the people in general. The Lord desires to have in his service order and discipline, not excitement and confusion. We are not now able to describe with accuracy the scenes to be enacted in our world in the future; but this we know, that this is a time when we must watch unto prayer; for the great day of the Lord is at hand. Satan is rallying his forces. We need to be thoughtful and still, and to contemplate the truths of revelation. Excitement is not favorable to growth in grace, to true purity and sanctification of spirit. . . .

"God calls upon His people to walk with sobriety and consistency. They should be very careful not to misrepresent and dishonor the holy doctrines of truth by strange performances, by confusion and tumult. By this, unbelievers are led to think that Seventh-day Adventists are a set of fanatics. Thus prejudice is created that prevents souls from receiving the message for this time. When believers speak the truth as it is in Jesus, they reveal a highly, sensible calm, not a storm of confusion. . . The things you have described as taking place in Indiana, the Lord has shown me would take place just before the close of probation. Every uncouth thing will be demonstrated, there will be shouting, with drums, music, and dancing. The senses of rational beings will become so confused that they cannot be trusted to make right decisions. And this is called the moving of the Holy Spirit. . . . Satan works amid the din and confusion of such music, which, if properly conducted, would be a praise and glory to God. He makes its effect like the poison string of the serpent.

"Those things which have been in the past will be in the future. Satan will make music a snare by the way in which it is conducted. The Holy Spirit never reveals itself in such methods, in such a bedlam of noise. This is an invention of Satan to cover up his ingenious methods for making of none effect the pure, sincere, elevating, ennobling, sanctifying truth for this time. Better never have the worship of God blended with music than to use musical instruments to do the work which last January was represented to me would be brought into our camp meetings. A bedlam of noise shocks the senses and perverts that which if conducted aright might be a blessing. The powers of satanic agencies blend with the din and noise, to have a carnival, and this is termed the Holy Spirit's working. . . No encouragement should be given to this kind of worship" (White: 2SM 35-38).

Another concern in the issue of worship is that of decorum. There seems to be concern over outbursts of praise, or concern over those who sway back and forth, waving their hands to the music. While these may be legitimate concerns, only God knows for sure who is genuine and who is not. I can recall one Christmas when my family had gathered for the holidays, my mother asked my sisters and me to make a tape of songs that we used to sing while growing up. She wanted to send it to a church member who loved to hear us sing. We all gathered around the tape recorder and began singing songs that brought back many memories. When we began to sing *"When We All Get To Heaven"* my mother became so moved at the thought of God's goodness to her, and how He had spared her life to see another Christmas (she had been at death's door several times during the year), she burst into a litany of praise, clapping her hands while shedding tears of joy.

In reflecting upon this scene, I could not help but think how such a response in some congregations might be interpreted as inappropriate. This response was not for show; it was in a home setting. It was a genuine heart-felt response of gratitude to God for His goodness and mercy. When others behave in like manner in church, what are your thoughts? Do you condemn them? Do you know what is the motivation behind such behavior? Since the enemy has indeed planted tares among the wheat, how can we know the genuine from the counterfeit? We simply are unable to judge the motives of others. **GOD SAYS. . .**

1 Samuel 16:7	*"For man looketh on the outward appearance, but the LORD looketh on the heart."*
Matthew 7:1,2	*"JUDGE NOT, that ye be not judged. For with what judgment ye judge, ye shall be judged. . . ."*
1 Thessalonians 5:19	*"Quench not the Spirit."*

It is only "by their fruits" that we can tell whether or not one is sincere and truly converted. Spirituality and Christian principles will be characteristic of the behavior not only in worship, but in the home, in the work place, or in any other environment.

Because God places importance upon worship, the instructions that He gave to the Israelites on how to prepare for worship, how to conduct worship, how to dress for worship, and how to behave in worship still apply in principle to us today. "So the priests were not to enter the sanctuary with shoes upon their feet. . . . They were to leave their shoes in the court before entering the sanctuary, and also to wash both their hands and their feet before ministering in the tabernacle or at the alter of burnt-offering. Thus was constantly taught the lesson that all defilement must be put away from those who would approach into the presence of God. . . Everything connected with the apparel and deportment of the priests was to be such as to impress the beholder with a sense of the holiness of God, the sacredness of his worship, and the purity required of those who came into his presence" (White: PP 350, 351). **GOD SAYS. . .**

Exodus 19:10-13

"And the LORD Said unto Moses, Go unto the people, and sanctify them today and tomorrow, and let them wash their clothes, And be ready. . . And thou shalt set bounds unto the people round about . . . There shall not an hand touch it, but he shall surely be stoned or shot through; whether it be beast or man, it shall not live. . . ."

Leviticus 26:2

"AND Ye shall reverence my sanctuary: I am the Lord."

Numbers 1:50, 51

"But thou shalt appoint the Levites over the tabernacle of testimony, and over all the vessels thereof, and over all things that belong to it. . . and they shall minister unto it. . . and the stranger that cometh nigh shall be put to death."

Psalm 95:6

"O come, let us worship and bow down: let us kneel before the LORD our maker."

Psalm 29:2

"Give unto the LORD the glory due unto His name; worship the LORD in the beauty of holiness."

Psalm 30:4	*"Sing unto the LORD, o ye saints of his, and give thanks at the remembrance of his holiness."*
Psalm 46:10	*"Be still, and know that I am God . . . ."*
Psalm 100:2, 4	*"Serve the Lord with gladness: come before His presence with singing. Enter into His gates with thanksgiving, and into His courts with praise: be thankful unto him, and bless his name."*
Psalm 116:18	*"I will pay my vows unto the LORD now in the presence of all His people."*
Ecclesiastes 5:1, 2	*"KEEP THY foot when thou goest to the house of God, and be more ready to hear, than to give the sacrifice of fools: for they consider not rash with thy mouth, and let not thine heart be hasty to utter any thing before God; therefore let thy words be few."*
Isaiah 1:12-20	*"When ye come to appear before me, who hath required this at your hand, to tread my courts? Bring no more vain oblations. . . the calling of assemblies, I cannot away with; it is iniquity, even the solemn meeting. Your new moons and your appointed feasts my soul hateth: they are a trouble unto me; I am weary to bear them. And when ye spread forth your hands, I will hide mine eyes from you: yea, when ye make many prayers, I will not hear: your hands are full of blood. Wash you, make you clean; put away the evil of your doings from before mine eyes; cease to do evil' Learn to do well; seek judg ment, relieve the oppressed, judge the fatherless, plead for the widow. Come, let*

us reason together. . . . If ye be willing and obedient, ye shall eat the good of the land: But if ye refuse and rebel, ye shall be devoured with the sword: for the mouth of the LORD hath spoken it."

Isaiah 32:17, 18

"*And the work of righteousness shall be peace; and the effect of righteousness quietness and assurance forever. And my people shall dwell in a peaceable habitation, and in sure dwellings, and in quiet resting places.*"

Habbakkuk 2:20

"*But the LORD is in his holy temple: let all the earth keep silence before him.*"

Zechariah 2:13

"*Be silent, O all flesh, before the LORD. . . .*"

Matthew 6:5-7

"*And when thou prayest, thou shalt not be as the hypocrites are: for they love to pray standing in the synagogues and in the corners of the streets, that they may be seen of men. . . But when ye pray, use not vain repetitions. . . .*"

John 4:24

"*God is a spirit: and they that worship him must worship him in spirit and in truth.*"

The concept of *reverence* is generally thought of in terms of behavior in the sanctuary. Acts such as chewing gum, carrying on conversations throughout the service, or walking in and out of the service are generally deemed to be irreverent. "The [Israelites] were to be impressed that everything connected with the service of God must be regarded with the greatest reverence. Their person and their clothing must be freed from impurity" (White: PP 303).

Since music plays such a vital role in worship and can influence behavior for good or bad, it is necessary to choose that which will not only be edifying (this is very crucial to a meaningful worship experience), but will also engender appropriate behavior. "God's work is ever characterized by calmness and dignity. We cannot afford to sanction anything that would bring in confusion and weaken our zeal in regard to the great work that God has given us to do in the world to prepare for the second coming of Christ" (White: 2SM 41).

There are two categories of music that must be considered—the *liturgical* which is *functional* service music, and *non-liturgical* music which is based upon religious themes but is *not intended for worship*. The latter category of songs seems to be a primary element in the music controversy. Albeit some might adamantly hold to the belief that it is all right to use non-liturgical music in worship to liven things up, in principle, it is unacceptable to God. He will only accept that which is offered according to His instructions. We must approach Him on His own terms. Scripture has given us examples of those whose attitudes and behavior were not acceptable to God:

Genesis 4:3,4	*"Cain brought of the fruit of the ground an offering unto the LORD. And Abel, he brought of the firstlings of his flock and of the fat thereof. And the LORD had respect unto Abel and to his offering: But unto Cain and to his offering he had no respect...."*
Exodus 32:7,8,19	*"And the LORD said... thy people which thou broughtest out of the land of Egypt, have corrupted themselves... they have made them a molten calf, and have worshiped it, and have sacrificed thereunto... He [Moses] saw the calf, and the dancing...."*
1 Kings 18:28	*"And they cried aloud, and cut themselves after their manner with knives and lancets, til the blood gushed out upon them...."*
Jeremiah 2:11	*"But my people have changed their glory for that which doth not profit...."*
Jeremiah 7:30	*"For the children of Judah have done evil in my sight, saith the LORD: they have set*

their abominations in the house which is called by my name, to pollute it."

Mark 7:7 "*Howbeit in vain do they worship me, teaching for doctrines the commandments of men.*"

"The psalmist describes the effect produced upon the worshiper by the adoration of idols. . . Man will rise no higher than his conceptions of truth, purity, and holiness. If the mind is never exalted above the level of humanity, if it is not uplifted by faith to contemplate infinite wisdom and love, the man will be constantly sinking lower and lower. The worshippers of false gods clothed their deities with human attributes and passions, and thus their standard of character was degraded to the likeness of sinful humanity. They were defiled in consequence" (White: PP 91).

Summary

True worship comes as a result of having had a personal encounter with God whether it be out in nature, in the "secret closet," in a small group, or in a corporate setting; it is not contingent upon the labyrinth of external elements (culture, style, music, the ritual itself, etc.) in order for it to occur. Jesus said that our motives and attitudes *(spirit)*, coupled with Biblical principles *(truth)*, form the basis of true worship.

CHAPTER EIGHT

MUSIC MINISTRY

The origin of music ministry can be traced back to the time when God instructed the Israelites to build a sanctuary so that He could "dwell among them" (Exodus 25:8). Only the Levites were "appointed to all manner of service of the tabernacle of the house of God" (1 Chronicles 6:48). In building this sanctuary nothing was left to chance, not even the music. The books of the Chronicles give details regarding the organizational structure of the musicians and their roles, and citations of the instruments used in worship:

1 Chronicles 25:7

"Brethren. . . were instructed in the songs of the Lord, even all that were cunning. . . ."

1 Chronicles 6:31, 32, 48

"And these are they. . . set over the service of song in the house of the LORD . . . And they ministered before the tabernacle of the congregation with singing. . . and then they waited on their office according to their order. . . The Levites were appointed unto all manner of service of the tabernacle of the house of God."

1 Chronicles 9:13,27,33	*"Very able men for the work of the services of the house of God. . . And they lodged around about the house of God because the charge was upon them. . . The singers. . . were employed in that work day and night."*
1 Chronicles 15:19,22	*"So the singers . . . were appointed. . . And Chenaniah . . . instructed about the song because he was skilful."*
1 Chronicles 23:5	*"Moreover. . . four thousand praised the LORD with the instruments which I made, said David, to praise therewith."*
1 Chronicles 25:7	*"So the number of them. . . that were instructed in the songs of the LORD, even all that were cunning, was two hundred fourscore and eight."*
2 Chronicles 23:13	*"The singers with instruments of music, and such as taught to sing praise. . . ."*

From these verses one can see that the Biblical prerequisites for music ministry were *training and preparation*. This solemn responsibility was not carelessly entrusted to just anyone. Today, however, this is not always the case. I have witnessed or experienced situations wherein the music of some services of the church was left entirely to chance. In such cases the volunteer musicians scheduled were not committed to their responsibility and would either come unprepared, come late, or not come at all. There are situations that you may even be able to identify with, including those wherein some persons with exceptional talent become arrogant and unteachable, and the spirit of pride that they have developed renders them unavailable for service except on special occasions or when big audiences are involved. "Music is acceptable to God only when the heart is sanctified and made soft and holy by its facilities. But many who delight in music know nothing of making melody in their hearts to the Lord. Their heart is gone after their idols" (White: Ev 512).

Competition among musicians is also prevalent. I can recall that once, while conducting a workshop, this issue surfaced. One of the major concerns voiced was that of when a musician who may not be as gifted, but faithfully serves the church, is pushed aside on special occasions and another musician is brought in. Such situations foster attitudes and behavior that not only cause dissension, but are disruptive to the music program of the church. This is also an insult to God, for not only is it to Him that the musical offering should be directed (not the congregation), but the confusion caused by the conflict does not glorify Him. To this, **GOD SAYS...**

Deuteronomy 15:21   *"And if there be any blemish therein. . . thou shalt not sacrifice it unto the LORD thy God."*

2 Samuel 23:3, 4   *"He that ruleth over men must be just, ruling in the fear of God."*

There are two aspects of music ministry. The first is the administrative or business part which involves working closely with the pastor and serving on committees for the planning, coordinating, and scheduling music for the various services, including weddings and funerals; maintaining the instruments and other equipment; overseeing the budget, and the list goes on. Speaking of maintenance of instruments (pianos especially), this is an area that is greatly neglected in many churches. All pianos, whether new or old, need to be tuned at least every six months. The different playing styles, and the changes in temperature and humidity can seriously damage the instruments over a period of time.

Another problematic area is that of copyright infringement. Because many churches do not have a budget for purchasing music, they will copy music without permission. According to the law, this is theft, and music publishers are becoming intolerant of churches and schools that break the law. Stiff fines (as much as $10,000 or more) have already been imposed upon perpetrators. Pastors and ministers of music should be knowledgeable of copyright laws and should do everything possible to comply with them. The Library of Congress will have current information regarding copyright laws. The address can be obtained from your local library.

Music ministry, however, means far more than attending to the business aspect. It is a position designed by God for the purpose of leading the congregation into a worship experience that is both meaningful and edifying, whatever the service. Anyone who participates in the musical activities of the church can be considered a minister of music, whether choir director, choir member, chorister, organist, instrumentalist, or vocalist (the ministry of singing will be discussed in more detail in Chapter Nine). Let's discuss these roles and their impact upon worship.

The choir is an important aspect of music ministry. Webster defines it as "an organized company of singers. . . devoted to the order's special work." Its primary function is to provide music for the service and facilitate in leading the congregation in singing the hymns. However, the latter does not always occur. There are existing situations whereby the choir will have no idea what the hymns will be until they are announced. Whenever an unfamiliar hymn is selected that neither the choir nor the congregation is able to sing, there always seems to be an uncomfortable feeling looming in the air followed by a sense of relief when the ordeal is over. How can God possibly be glorified or the church edified under these conditions?

Factors that can seriously undermine the effectiveness of the choir ministry are poor attendance at rehearsals; tardiness for appointments; not showing up to sing after having attended the rehearsal; showing up to sing without having rehearsed; unfriendly attitudes toward members; clamoring for solos; forming cliques; voicing opinions that dampen enthusiasm, and the list goes on. "I was taken into some of your singing exercises, and was made to read the feelings that existed in the company. . . . There were petty jealousies, envy, evil surmising, and evil speaking. . . . The heart service is what God requires; the forms and lip service are as sounding brass and tinkling cymbal. Your singing is for display, not to praise God with the spirit and understanding. The state of the heart reveals the quality of the religion of the professor of godliness" (White: Ev 507).

As ministers of music then, choir members are responsible for being examples to the congregation in attitude, deportment, and lifestyle that are consistent with the privilege of ministry. The enthusiasm with which the anthems and hymns are sung, reading the Scripture, being alert and attentive to the sermon all have an impact upon one's worship experience. The music which God's people sing has eternal value and should be treated as such.

In order to be an effective spiritual leader in worship, it is necessary for the choir director to daily "experience God's saving grace and redeeming work in his/her life,. . . understand the place of music in the life of the believer and in the worship of the church, . . . [and]. . . develop the skills necessary for self-expression" (Osbeck: 5). As a professional, the director must be a competent musician, one who can read and interpret music; one who knows how to choose music that will accentuate the strengths of the choir; and one who is prepared for the service. This applies to children's choirs as well. It is imperative to choose music that is appropriate for their level of understanding (not songs that deal with "adult" situations), and to protect their delicate voices from being damaged as a result of singing unsuitable music.

Choristers have the responsibility of directing the singing in the absence of a choir director. Not only should this officer possess the talent for singing, but should also know how to lead the congregation in a meaningful worship experience that will be edifying, and conduct the hymns in a way that will not be distracting. "Music can be a great power for good, yet we do not make the most of this branch of worship. The singing is generally done from impulse or to meet special cases, and at other times those who sing are left to blunder along, and the music loses its proper effect upon the minds of those present. Music should have beauty, pathos, and power. Let the voices be lifted in songs of praise and devotion. Call to your aid, if practicable, instrumental music, and let the glorious harmony ascend to God, and acceptable offering" (White: 4T 70).

The chorister should conduct in a way that will not be distracting to the organist or pianist, and should coordinate the hymns with these musicians ahead of time in order to avoid embarrassing them by calling hymns that are difficult to play without practice. This can be very unnerving and demoralizing to the musicians.

By nature of the instrument, the organist is one of the most important musicians of the church, and is the one who can make the difference between a service running smoothly or very poorly. It is imperative then that anyone who assumes this responsibility understands and knows how to play the instrument, knows how to read music, is able to sing, and is proficient at leading the congregation in the singing of the hymns, especially in churches where there is no choir.

By design, the organ is the primary instrument of worship and is therefore supposed to accompany congregational singing alone, but it is often coupled with the piano for various reasons. This being the case, the organist and pianist should coordinate the music so that they sound unified and not as though they are fighting when playing together. The musicians, unfortunately, are often placed at an unfair disadvantage because they do not always know in advance what the hymns will be. Hence, they cannot practice them. This situation not only promotes mediocrity in playing, but is often the underlying cause of discord and competition between the musicians.

When it comes to the use of instruments, the requirement is the same—preparation and humility, both of which are essential to effective music ministry. "Display is not religion nor sanctification. There is nothing more offensive in God's sight than a display of instrumental music when those taking part are not consecrated, are not making melody in their hearts to the Lord. The offering most sweet and acceptable in God's sight is a heart made humble by self-denial, by lifting the cross and following Jesus. We have no time to spend in seeking those things that only please the senses. Close heart searching is needed. With tears and heartbroken confession we need to draw nigh to God that He may draw nigh to us" (White: Ev 510).

If indeed music is as important to worship as are prayer and the spoken word, then every effort should be made to secure and compensate the best musicians possible. According to the Bible, **GOD SAYS...**

Numbers 18:24	*"But the tithes of the children of Israel, which they offer as an heave offering unto the LORD, I have given to the Levites to inherit. . . ."*
Nehemiah 12:47	*"Nehemiah gave the portions of the singers and the porters, every day his portion: and they sanctified holy things unto the Levites. . . ."*
Luke 10:7	*"The labourer is worthy of his hire. . . ."*

I am deeply concerned over the fact that this Biblical principle is not always implemented within the Seventh-day Adventist Church. What is the purpose of our colleges and universities conferring music degrees upon their graduates, only to force the vast majority of them to seek employment as "well-paid" ministers of music in other denominations because there is no provision for them within the church structure? Why should churches, expecially the small congregations, have to suffer want of a trained musician? Although emphasis is placed upon preaching and teaching, (both of which will perish at the second coming of Jesus Christ) should not the ministers also be familiar with the basics of this "tool of the trade"—music ministry? Since it is only music that will be a part of our experience both on earth and in heaven, should not the situation be reversed?

Another concern is that for the exceptionally talented musicians who want to remain faithful to the church, yet who feel compelled to develop and grow musically. Because there is no place for them to serve as professional musicians within the church, they are forced to make one of two painful decisions—to pursue a musical career outside of the church, or remain in the church and bury their talents. Because this Biblical principle has been neglected, the enemy has been given an opportunity to take advantage of the situation. "When there has been a departure from the right path, it is difficult to return. Barriers have been removed, safeguards broken down. One step in the wrong direction prepares the way for another. . . The last deviation from right and principle will lead to separation from God and may end in apostasy. . . Whatever a man becomes accustomed to, be it influence for good or evil, he finds it difficult to abandon" (White: 4T 578).

Summary

The primary goal of music ministry is that of *edifying* the church. The effectiveness of this ministry depends upon one's understanding of the importance of music in worship, of which preparation and training are key factors. Anyone who participates in the musical activities of the church, whether chorister, vocalist, instrumentalist, organist, choir director, or choir member is a minister of music, and should be a devout Christian, a competent musician, and able to work with people.

When God gave Moses the blueprint to build the earthly sanctuary, nothing was left to chance; every detail of the service was addressed. Music ministry was so important to God that He did not permit just anyone to serve in that capacity; only trained musicians from the tribe of Levi. Holy Writ records that the musicians were employed and paid from the tithe. By failing to adhere to the principles of music ministry as outlined in God's Word, the church has sown the wind and is now reaping the whirlwind of confusion and controversy. *"Now these things happened unto them for ensamples; and they are written for our admonition. . . ."* (1 *Corinthians 10:11)* . . . May God's will be done on earth as it is in heaven.

CHAPTER NINE

SINGING IN WORSHIP

O f all the musical instruments that exist today, the human voice is the only one created by God Himself. Therefore, the talent of singing is a gift that should be used to glorify His name. After all, that is the purpose for which we were created.

Because singing is so natural, usually little or no thought is given to how the vocal mechanism works. Although it may seem that singing merely involves opening the mouth to release the sound, the process of producing musical tones is more complex than that, for it involves the use of vibrating vocal chords, the soft palate, the tongue, the mouth, the bones under the eyes (masque), the breastplate, the nape of the neck, the top of the head, the lungs, and of course, the diaphragm. With all that is involved in singing, training the voice is very important and should not be neglected. "In all our work more attention should be given to the culture of the voice. We may have knowledge, but unless we know how to use the voice correctly, our work will be a failure. . . The truth must not be marred by being communicated through defective utterance. . . And by the music of [one's] voice and the emphasis placed on the words [one] can make the scene presented stand out as clearly before the mind of the listener as if it could actually be seen" (White: 6T 380-381).

The voice is more than an instrument—it is a tool for ministry, and with this gift of song come the obligation and responsibility of singing in a manner that will be edifying to the listener. "We should endeavor in our songs of praise to approach as nearly as possible to the harmony of the heavenly choirs. I have often been pained to hear untrained voices, pitched to the highest key, literally shrieking the sacred words of some hymn of praise. How inappropriate those sharp, rasping voices for the solemn, joyous worship of God. I long to stop my ears, or flee from the place, and I rejoice when the painful exercise is ended. Those who make singing a part of divine worship should select hymns with music appropriate to the occasion, not funeral notes, but cheerful, yet solemn melodies. The voice can and should be modulated, softened, and subdued" (White: Ev 507-508).

When the Israelites brought their animal sacrifices before the Lord they were to be without spot or blemish. When we present our talents to God as a living sacrifice, He requires no less of us now than He did the Israelites. "He who has bestowed upon us all the gifts that enable us to be workers together with God, expects His servants to cultivate their voices, so that they can speak and sing in a way that all can understand. It is not loud singing that is needed, but clear intonation, correct pronunciation, and distinct utterance. Let all take time to cultivate the voice, so that God's praise can be sung in clear, soft tones, not with harshness and shrillness that offend the ear. The ability to sing is the gift of God; let it be used to His glory" (White: 9T 143).

Because this magnificent instrument is housed in the human body, great care should be taken toward cultivating and maintaining a healthy lifestyle. This philosophy has captured the attention of many in today's society. Newspapers, magazines, TV talk shows, and other media continuously report on scientific research and discoveries of the merits of a diet high in fruits and vegetables. Stress is placed upon exercising and lowering fat intake in order to prevent cholesterol buildup and subsequent strokes, heart attacks, or even death. All of these issues are directly related to singing and to salvation. "Those who transgress the law of God in their physical organism, will be inclined to violate the law of God spoken from Sinai" (White: CDF 17).

As in the parable of the talents, God expects a return on the gifts and abilities that He has bestowed upon us. This cannot happen with clogged minds or impaired physical health which is a ploy of Satan to divert our attention from spiritual things. If we follow the divinely appointed rules for health we will be spared from disease and premature death. "Our first duty toward God and our fellow beings is that of self-development. Every faculty with which the Creator has endowed us should be cultivated to the highest degree of perfection that we may be able to do the greatest amount of good of which we are capable. Hence that time is spent to good account which is used in the establishment and preservation of physical and mental health. We cannot afford to dwarf or cripple any function of body or mind. As surely as we do this, we must suffer the consequences" (White: CDF 15).

There are not only rules for maintaining physical health but there are also rules for maintaining vocal health as well. For example, one should stay in the normal comfort range of singing (tessitura) and should not scream. It is very disconcerting to hear many of today's popular artists abusing their voices this way, all for entertainment. I am especially alarmed over the fact that the perpetuation of incorrect or "bad" singing is fostered through CDs, radio, and television. Youth are especially vulnerable, for as they become conditioned to those sounds that they like and try to imitate, they end up damaging their young voices. No encouragement should be given to this kind of singing. "I was shown that the youth must take a higher stand and make the work of God the man of their counsel and their guide. Solemn responsibilities rest upon the young, which they lightly regard. The introduction of music into their homes, instead of inciting to holiness and spirituality, has been the means of diverting their minds from the truth. Frivolous songs and the popular sheet music of the day seem congenial to their taste. . . Music, when not abused, is a great blessing; but when put to a wrong use, it is a terrible curse" (White: 1T 497).

Other suggestions for maintaining vocal health are to warm up the voice with vocal exercises before singing. Use physical exercises to relax (shoulder rolls, neck rolls, dangle arms, stretching, etc.). Get plenty of rest, and keep hydrated by drinking plenty of water. Dr. Thomas Cleveland, a physician at the Voice Center of Vanderbilt Medical Center in Nashville, Tennessee suggests that vegetarianism is preferable to meat-eating, and advises singers to avoid foods that produce heartburn such as fats, chocolate, caffeine, and alcohol. He said that as of 1994, scientific research revealed that heavy spices cause stomach cancer. Does this not sound familiar?

In worship, singing is just as important to the service as are prayer and the spoken word, and is the only component of music ministry in which all can participate. "God has chosen the melody of song as one of His tools for saving souls. It is one of the most effective ways in which to internalize the message of the gospel and other spiritual truths; help subdue rude and uncultivated natures; stimulate thought; engender sympathy; promote harmony of action; and banish the gloom and foreboding that destroy courage and weaken effort" (White: Ed 167). We are admonished to sing to the glory of God and to the edification of one another through *"hymns, psalms, and spiritual songs"* because each song type has a different function that nurtures and provides balance within the Christian experience.

Hymns are generally thought of as a collection of songs contained in a hymnal. They are, in essence, songs of praise and thanksgiving that are vertically directed from man to God. However, in this scenario, the psalms (scriptural translations) will represent the songs of praise while the hymns will symbolically represent the didactic aspect of ministry that is necessary for Christian growth. These are the doctrinal songs that reinforce the fundamentals of our beliefs. For example, hymns such as *"Don't Forget the Sabbath"* and *"Holy Day, Jehovah's Rest"* not only teach Sabbath observance, but that it was man, not God, who changed the Sabbath from the seventh day to the first day of the week. This is the reason why we do not use a Baptist, Catholic, or Methodist hymnal, etc., because some of the doctrines conflict with the beliefs of the Seventh-day Adventist Church.

Spiritual songs represent the horizontal testimonies, the songs of experience, directed from one to another about God's goodness, love, forgiveness, mercy, grace, and providence. They are songs of encouragement, for they tell of how God has worked within the life of the Christian. This is, in the truest sense of the word, the original idea and intent of gospel music—songs that tell the good news of salvation. Today, however, gospel music has come to mean a particular *style* or category of music. To illustrate this point I call to mind an experience that I had while visiting in Africa on a mission with Operation Reachback, Inc. One of my projects was that of presenting a choir concert as the grand finale to the short visit. After organizing a group of about forty-five persons I chose Negro Spirituals as the music. Many of them had never heard of these songs before, nor had they heard of the context in which they evolved. Take, for instance, the song, *"Lawd, how come me here, I wish I neve' wuz bo'n."* They did not understand the atrocities of slavery and the depths of despair that many slaves experienced. Therefore, before teaching each song I gave an explanation of its meaning. I observed, however, that although the music was performed very well and so beautifully, it sounded "different" because the African dialect did not coincide with the "broken English" that is so characteristic of spirituals. I then realized that the meaning of this music was foreign to them because it was not an experience that *they* could relate to.

When I pondered this situation I began to realize the powerful spiritual implication it had. I asked myself the question, 'how can one sing or play "the Lord's song", to the glory of God, without first having an experience with Him? Perhaps this is how and why the expression "singing/playing for show"came into existence. Perhaps this is why congregations do not sing very enthusiastically any more, and if so, they sing that way only on songs that they like or on songs that do not prick the conscience. Sacred music that is deemed lifeless and dead (as it is so often perceived by some) could very well be the result of an empty Christian life—not having an experience with the Lord. This is why we are admonished to sing/play with understanding so that we and others may be truly edified. When one is connected to God, even those songs with a slower pace can and will be sung with life and vitality—it's a matter of experience.

"When human beings sing with the Spirit and the understanding, heavenly musicians take up the strain, and join in the song of thanksgiving. . . It is not loud singing that is needed, but clear intonation, correct pronunciation, and distinct utterance. . . so that God's praise can be sung in clear, soft tones, not with harshness and shrillness that offend the ear. The ability to sing is the gift of God; let it be used to His glory" (White: 9T 143, 144).

The congregation should be given every opportunity to sing, and should sing with gusto. The enthusiasm generated will be contagious, and soon all will find themselves raising their voices in praise to God. "I saw that all should sing with the spirit and with the understanding also.

The nearer the people of God can approach to correct harmonious singing, the more is he glorified, the church benefitted, and unbelievers favorably affected" (White: 1T 146). **GOD SAYS...**

Psalm 30:4

"Sing unto the LORD . . . and give thanks at the remembrance of his holiness."

Psalm 47:7

"Sing ye praises with understanding."

Psalm 96:1-3

"O SING unto the Lord a new song. . . Sing unto the Lord, bless His name; show forth his salvation from day to day. Declare his glory among the heathen, his wonders among all people."

Psalm 98:5, 6

"Sing unto the Lord with the harp, and the voice of a psalm. With trumpets and sound of cornet make a joyful noise before the LORD, the King."

Psalm 104: 33

"I will sing unto the LORD as long as I live: I will sing praise to my God while I have my being."

Colossians 3:16

"Let the word of Christ dwell in you richly in all wisdom; teaching and admonishing one another in psalms and hymns and spiritual songs, singing with grace in your hearts to the Lord."

Therefore, the music that we select as church musicians should provide variety and balance as we help to nurture our congregations in their spiritual growth. Individuals who sing should choose music with substantive lyrics, preferably based upon Scripture, and should avoid those songs with "hooks and lines" (recurring phrases designed to stick in the mind) because that is a commercial gimmick used by the music industry to *sell* songs. When interpreting a song the singer should consider the mood and the type—prayer, praise, testimony, etc., and communicate that sentiment. Ornamentation should be used for emphasis, not for display, and should cause the listener to *think* about what is being said rather than evoking a thoughtless reaction to the vocal skills of the singer.

"Great improvement can be made in singing. Some think that the louder they sing the more music they make; but noise is not music. Good singing is like the music of the birds—subdued and melodious. In some of our churches I have heard solos that were altogether unsuitable for the service of the Lord's house. The long drawn-out notes and the peculiar sounds (common in operatic singing) are not pleasing to the angels. They delight to hear the simple songs of praise sung in a natural tone. The songs in which every word is uttered clearly, in a music tone, are the songs that they join us in singing. They take up the refrain that is sung from the heart with the spirit and the understanding" (White: Ev 510).

"If the [music] is of an emotional character, it will affect the feelings, but not the heart and conscience. Such [music] results in no lasting good, but it often wins the hearts of the people and calls out their affections for the man who pleases them" (White: 5T 301).

The gift of song was given to humanity to render praise and adoration unto God, not to foster pride and ambition for display. When this happens the singer and those who are being entertained have little thought of the worship of God and often forget Him. However, when we seek to glorify Him and not ourselves, He will tangibly bless our efforts and will in turn allow some of His glory to shine upon us as we minister to others.

Summary

God has created the greatest instrument of all—the human voice. And, as with all manufacturers, instruction manuals via His Word and the Spirit of Prophecy have been provided for the proper use, care, and maintenance of the instrument. A lifetime warranty is guaranteed if these principles are diligently observed. When He returns He will require an explanation of what, when, where, why, how, and for whom this talent was used.

CHAPTER TEN

INSTRUMENTS IN WORSHIP

The first Biblical reference to musical instruments is found in Genesis 4:21 which names Jubal as *"the father of all such as handled the harp and organ."* Subsequent references include some of the instruments that we now identify as woodwinds: the flute (ugab) and oboe (chaleh); brass: the trumpet or cornet (chasoserah), horn (shophar); strings: the lyre (kinnor), the harp (nebel), the zither (kithara, a ten-stringed lyre), and psaltry; and percussion: the tambourine (timbrel), cymbals (selseliml), castanets (sistrum) and drums (tabrets), just to name a few *(SDA Bible Dictionary)*. "The use of musical instruments is not at all objectionable. These were used in religious services in ancient times. The worshippers praised God upon the harp and cymbal, and music should have its place in our services. It will add to the interest" (White: Ev 500-501).

Instruments are grouped into families or categories generally by the way in which they produce sound and by the material from which they are made. For example, woodwinds (reed aerophones) are wind instruments that require covering holes to produce sound. Brass (aerophones) are also wind instruments that, with the exception of the trombone which uses a slide, require depressing valves to produce sound. Strings (chordophones) are instruments that are plucked or bowed; and percussion (idiophones and membranophones) are either pitched or non-pitched instruments that are struck or shaken.

Although the Bible sanctions the use of instruments, there are those who are of the opinion that some are "good" and some are "bad." I submit to you, however, that instruments in and of themselves are neither good nor bad, and that any instrument can be used for good or evil. The spiritual condition of the heart of the musician is what produces the "good" or "bad" fruit, for *"out of the abundance of the heart the mouth speaketh"* (Matthew 12:34). "No one who has an indwelling Savior will dishonor Him before others by producing strains from a musical instrument which call the mind from God and heaven to light and trifling things" (White: 1T 510).

Today, drums seem to be the most controversial of all instruments, perhaps because of the way in which they are played; because they traditionally are not considered to be a "church" instrument; because they are associated with conjuring up evil spirits; or even because they were created into Lucifer's anatomical structure (See Ezekiel 28:13). You might even think of other reasons not mentioned here. These reasons, unfortunately, often result in throwing the baby out with the bath water.

The myth that drums are evil originated from European missionaries who went to Africa and could not relate to the culture. Africa was nicknamed the "Dark Continent" not only because of the skin color of its inhabitants, but "mostly because the outside world knew very little about the geography and peoples of this vast land mass, particularly in the area south of the Sahara Desert" (Titon: 64). Drums were and still are an integral part of African culture. However, because the missionaries did not understand the intricacies of playing them, and because they were sometimes used in voodoo and other rites involving spiritualism, they were deemed evil. Failing to deal with African music on its own terms led the missionaries to substitute these traditions for European standards. Consequently, this acculturation attempted to strip Africans of one of the most important elements of their culture.

By observation one can see that all drums are not created equal and that they all do not have the same function. For example, authentic African drums are constructed from wood and animal skins. "They may be played at religious ceremonies or social gatherings, traditional dances for children's games, for work, and for war" (Jones: 146). They are also used as a tool for communicating messages. In North and South America, the water-drum, also made of wood and animal skin, is prevalent in Navajo and Apache cultures. Even in India drumming is important to the texture of performance (Titon: 54, 248).

In western music, however, there are two categories of drums—pitched (timpani, steel drums, tom-toms, etc.) and non-pitched (snare, bongos, drum kit often referred to as a trap set, etc.). The "drum kit" (bass, tom-toms, snare, suspended cymbal, hi-hat, etc.), a descendant of European military and marching band instruments, is the source of contention today. In the 1920s jazz drummers experimented with one person playing several instruments, feet included. As technology and technique improved over the ensuing years, the drum kit became one of the main components of popular music, rock bands, jazz ensembles, and even gospel music. In light of this, the remainder of this discussion will be in reference to the drum kit, and the principles cited will also apply to electronic instruments—synthesizers, drum machines, and all others that reproduce the sound of acoustic instruments.

Of the three main elements of music—rhythm, melody, and harmony—rhythm is the one element that offers immediate satisfaction, and does not require the degree of thought and contemplation that melody and harmony do. The characteristic feature of drums and other percussion instruments in today's music is that of accentuating the beat, thus overpowering the melody and all other elements. Scientific research has proven that when the tension and release of music is rapid it appeals more to the physical. Conversely, when the tension and release span progress at a slower rate the mind is more actively involved. This is why young people naturally gravitate toward music that is fast or has a driving beat, in addition to the fact that it is contemporary—that which is meaningful and relevant to them; that which they can understand. It stands to reason that if one wants God to control the mind, it is difficult for Him to do so through a medium that accentuates the physical rather than the mental. "Satan knows what organs to excite to animate, engross, and charm the mind so that Christ is not desired. The spiritual longings of the soul for divine knowledge, for growth in grace, are wanting" (White: 1T 497).

As I mentioned earlier, many instruments were used to celebrate religious, secular, and military events, personal use, and worship during antiquity. It is especially interesting to note, however, that of the many instruments listed in the Bible, timbrels (drums) were not included among those cited for use in the sanctuary.

1 Chronicles 15:28	"Thus all Israel brought up the ark with . . . the cornet and with trumpets, and with cymbals, making a noise with psaltreies and harps."
1 Chronicles 16:4, 5, 42	"And he [David] appointed certain of the Levites to minister before the ark . . . with psaltreies and with harps; but Asaph made a sound with cymbals. . . with trumpets and cymbals. . . and with musical instruments of God."
2 Chronicles 29:25, 27	"And he [Hezekiah, the King] set the Levites in the house of the LORD with cymbals, with psaltreies, and with harps according to the commandments of David. . . with the trumpets, and with instruments ordained by David King of Israel."
2 Chronicles 5:11, 12	"When the priests were come out of the holy place. . . the Levites. . . having cymbals and psaltreies and harps. . . and with them an hundred and twenty priests sounding with trumpets. . . ."
Psalm 33:2, 3	"Praise the LORD with the harp: sing unto him with the psaltrey and instruments of ten strings. . . Play skilfully with a loud noise."

One possible explanation for not using drums could be that by nature, the drum is not a melodic instrument. Throughout the Bible there are numerous references to singing and making "melody" with the voice and with instruments, which drums are incapable of doing. Therefore,

Holy Writ does not record them as having been used in the sanctuary. Speaking of making melody, "rap" music, like the drum, is not melodic; it is rhythmic speech—the counterfeit of singing. Another possible explanation for not using them could be that God, looking through the annals of time, could foresee that the issue of the use of drums would be problematic because they are the main ingredient of commercial music, and hence, He established a precedent whereby their use was not a part of sacred worship. This, however, does not mean that drums are bad or evil. On the contrary, drums can indeed be effectively used when *orchestrated* under controlled conditions, and when used for *"color"*. However, that is usually not the case. They are generally played "by ear" and engaged from the beginning to the end of a piece as if they were a melodic instrument. The very loud volume which accents the weak beats, is often uncomfortable to the listener. As will be discussed in Chapter Twelve, the volume and the accentuation of these weak beats have scientifically been proven to be detrimental to the body—God's temple. To this **GOD SAYS...**

Romans 12:1	*"I BESEECH you therefore, brethren, by the mercies of God, that ye present your bodies a living sacrifice, holy, acceptable unto God, which is your reasonable service."*
1 Corinthians 3:16,17	*"Know ye not that ye are the temple of God, and that the Spirit of God dwelleth in you? If any man defile the temple of God, him shall God destroy; for the temple of God is holy, which temple ye are!"*
1 Corinthians 6:19,20	*"What? know ye not that your body is the temple of the Holy Ghost which is in you, which ye have of God, and ye are not your own? For ye are bought with a price: therefore glorify God in your body, and in your spirit, which are God's."*

"We are not to oppose the use of instrumental music in our work.

This part of the service is to be carefully conducted; for it is the praise of God in song" (White: 9T 144).

Summary

Holy Writ does not classify instruments as being "good" or "bad." Such human assessments often come as a result of the context in which they are associated, and these assessments are, in most instances, based upon one's background and experience. For example, there are those who feel that drums are "evil" because of their association with night clubs and how the music makes them feel; or because of the unholy lifestyles and music produced by some who play them; or even because of their association with spiritualism. In the case of spiritualism, if this is why drums are deemed "evil", then the pipe organ, king of instruments, must also be "evil", for it, too, is used in movie productions dealing with spiritualism. The Bach "Toccata and Fugue in D Minor" for organ is a well-known piece that has been used in this setting. How ludicrous it is to blame the instrument, an inanimate object, for the condition of the musician. It is not only the technical ability of the musician, but also the spiritual condition of the heart that ultimately produces fruit that is "good" or "evil."

God has sanctioned the use of instruments in our worship to Him, but He has instructed us to develop our talents by "getting understanding," "playing skillfully," "making melody," and making a "difference between the holy and the profane" (commercial). The object lesson of development in the parable of the talents teaches us this. If the manner in which drums are played is no different from that of commercial music, then they should not be used. Therefore, according to the Bible, it is necessary to get training in order to play an instrument (drums included) in a way that will *edify* the congregation. After all, is that not the purpose for the use of instruments in worship?

CHAPTER ELEVEN

THE "HOLY" DANCE

Dance plays a *functional* role in the lives of many people groups around the world. For example, there are dances for weddings, births, funerals, planting and harvesting crops, and many other events. While attending a banquet a few years ago, I watched youth from East Africa perform some of these dances. It was particularly intriguing to note that these youth had never been to their native country, yet, they had learned these dances from their parents who wanted to preserve their heritage and expose them to their culture. Other cultural dances that come to mind are those performed during the festive Bahamian Junkanoo celebration the day after Christmas (dating back to the days of slavery); or, as in New Orleans, a jazz band accompanying a funeral procession to and from the cemetery; or even the Zulu dances performed during Mardi Gras.

As a nation, the United States does not have a specific native or cultural dance because it is a melting pot for all nations, kindreds, tongues, and peoples. So when the term "dance" is used the general connotation is that of entertainment, for many are only fads that come and go with the passing of time (Soft shoe, Twist, Mashed potatoes, Disco, Jerk, House, and many more). Some religions, however, have adopted the use of the holy dance because of Biblical references to dancing. From what I have observed, many of the behavioral characteristics of secular dancing are transferred to the *holy dance*, and by the changing of a word or two of the lyrics here and there (O Jesus vs. O baby) to fit the environment—church or night club. Otherwise, the sound, the feelings, the emotions, the moods, and the behavior engendered by the music are the same (the "spirit" is only alive and well as long as there is music).

In researching the Biblical references to dancing, the very first one occurs in Exodus 15:20 when, after having crossed the Red Sea, Miriam and the other women took the timbrels (drums) and led the Israelite congregation in dancing and songs of praise to God for deliverance from Egyptian bondage. "The separation of men and women into distinct bands was an Egyptian custom, as likewise was the performance of dances by groups of men and women, who accompanied their steps with music" (*SDA Bible Commentary* VI 573). In light of this, it is clear that, while in Egypt, the Israelites adopted dancing into their culture as a result of the pagan influences to which they were exposed and subjected to for over four hundred years.

The phrase, "praise Him with the timbrel and dance," in Psalm 150:4 has been a point of controversy for quite some time. In order to defend or condone the "holy dance" there are those who use the argument that David "danced before the Lord," forgetting that he was in a parade of elders who were bringing the ark back to Jerusalem. This was indeed a *religious event*, a victory celebration, but not a worship service. Here, just as when David slayed Goliath, it was customary for the women to meet the returning armies with singing and dancing (See 1 Samuel 1:6; 2 Samuel 6:14-16). This is why Saul became so jealous of David when the women came out proclaiming *"Saul hath slain his thousands, and David his ten thousand"* (1 Samuel 18:7).

"David's dancing in reverent joy before God has been cited by pleasure-lovers in justification of the fashionable modern dance, but there is no ground for such an argument. In our day, dancing is associated with folly and midnight reveling. Health and morals are sacrificed to pleasure. By the frequenters of the ballroom, God is not an object of thought and reverence; prayer or the song of praise would be felt to be out of place in their assemblies. This test should be decisive. Amusements that have a tendency to weaken the love for sacred things and lessen our joy in the service of God, are not to be sought by Christians. The music and dancing in joyful praise to God at the removal of the ark had not the faintest resemblance to the dissipation of modern dancing. The one tended to the remembrance of God, and exalted His holy name. The other is a device of Satan to cause men to forget God and dishonor him" (White: PP 707).

The one reference to dancing in worship, however, is recorded in Exodus which describes the scene around the golden calf. The people were dancing and ended up naked and were almost repudiated by God. *"And the Lord said unto Moses, Go, get thee down; for thy people, which thou broughtest out of the land of Egypt, have corrupted themselves. . . Now therefore let me alone, that my wrath may wax hot against them, and that I may consume them. . . And he [Moses] saw the calf, and the dancing. . . [and] saw that the people were naked"* (Exodus 32:7,10,19,25).

Psalm 149 is an exhortation of praise to God for His love to the church—a body of people—and describes the daily circumstances, situations, and occasions for praising God—in the sanctuary; as Creator and King; upon their beds; with a two-edged sword when going to execute vengeance upon the heathen, etc. Psalm 150 appears to be a continuation of this exhortation, and merely describes some of the instruments that were used during that time.

In these two chapters, the word *"dance"* comes from the Hebrew word, *khalil*, which is referred to as *"pipe"* or "cornet"(check the reference in your Bible margin), and signifies an instrument such as a flute, the principal biblical *wind* instrument (Achtemeier 670). It was considered to be a joyful instrument and was associated with merrymaking and praise, and was often combined with the timbrel and the harp (the national instrument of the Hebrews) (Smith: 31). Therefore, in this context, the "dance" is referring to an instrument, not a physical activity.

Believe it or not, many of the activities, events, customs, and rituals recorded in Holy Writ are secular in nature, but are mistakenly interpreted as being "religious" simply because they appear in the Bible. Culture and tradition are often used to justify the use of "strange fire" in worship. The Bible speaks against adopting and sanctioning such rituals and other practices as sacred elements of worship (See Colossians 2:8). A frequent misconception is that religious activities mean worship. This is not necessarily the case. After consulting several different references on the subject, I noted that although Bible scholars say that dancing was a part of the secular and religious life of ancient Israel, not one text is cited for its use in sacred worship; they generally refer to the ones listed below (Achtemeier: 204). If you examine the contexts in which these references to dancing appear, you will see that some are secular in nature and do not occur within the context of sacred worship at all.

Exodus 15:20	*"Miriam. . . took a timbrel in her hand. . . and all the women went out after her with timbrels and with dances."*
Exodus 32:19,25	*"He saw the calf and the dancing. . . And Moses. . . saw that the people were naked. . . ."*
Judges 11:34	*"Jephthah came to Mizpeh. . . and behold, his daughter came out to meet him with timbrels and with dances. . . ."*
Judges 21:21	*"See, and behold, if the daughters of Shiloh come out to dance in dances. . . and catch you every man his wife. . . ."*
1 Samuel 18:6	*"The women came out of all cities of Israel singing and dancing, to meet king Saul, with tabrets. . . and with instruments of music."*
2 Samuel 6:14,16	*"And David danced before the LORD with all his might. . . and Michal Saul's daughter looked through a window, and saw king David leaping and dancing before the Lord; and she despised him in her heart."*
Psalm 68:22,25	*"I will bring my people again from the depths of the sea. . . The singers went before, the players on instruments followed after; among them were damsels playing with timbrels."*

Jeremiah 31:13	*"Then shall the virgin rejoice in the dance . . for I will turn their mourning into joy, and will comfort them, and make them rejoice from their sorrow."*
Matthew 14:6	*"The daughter of Herodias danced before them and pleased Herod."*
Luke 15:25	*"Now his elder son was in the field: and as he came and drew nigh to the house, he heard music and dancing."*

Today we live in a world in which our senses are constantly being bombarded with any and everything that will engender excitement. The same is true even in our worship. We tend to substitute man-made rites and rituals to fill a void and thus render ourselves vulnerable to the deceptions of the enemy. God wants us to exercise discipline and order in worship, not excitement and confusion. Anything less than this is a reproach to our faith and a dishonor to His name.

Summary

Dance in cultures around the world is generally a functional community activity that brings people together for various events. Even the Bible cites the different occasions in which dancing occurred, but it was never included as a part of sacred worship.

Unlike recreation, dancing as we know it is an element of entertainment which, by its very nature, is an amusement that has no redemptive value. To justify its use in worship on the basis of cultural or ethnic traditions is not scriptural but is a tactic of the enemy to use the music and noise, in the name of the Holy Spirit, to excite the passions and ultimately weaken interest in spiritual things, thus giving him an advantage over us that we will not be able to gainsay. No encouragement should be given to this kind of worship.

CHAPTER TWELVE

THE EFFECTS OF MUSIC UPON THE MIND AND THE BODY

S ound is an external stimulus that activates the senses through vibrations which produce mental images, memories, and physical responses, etc. It is the raw material from which music is derived. Music then is sound—*organized sound*, governed by time and space, that creates and influences one's feelings, ideas, emotions, moods, and behavior. Music results when the elements of rhythm, melody, harmony, timbre, and tempo are combined.

The human body is the epitome of musical expression, for all of the elements that make music what it is, we are, even down to our DNA (Deoxyribonucleic Acid). DNA, the substance that controls the development of all living things, contains four chemicals (Guanine, Cytosine, Thymine, and Adenine) that make up our generic code. Scientific research has discovered that these genes not only carry the blueprint for life but they also contain music (Humes: 8).

In 1982, I saw a CBS documentary on this very subject. Over forty years ago two scientists, Dr. James Watson (USA) and Dr. Francis Crick (UK) built a model of the structure of DNA. Normally the double helix is a vertical structure that has no resemblance to a musical staff. However, by using their imagination and thinking of it in musical terms, scientists have actually been able to see it as such. During the documentary, David Deamer, a piano-playing cell biologist from the University of California at Davis, demonstrated that when turned on its side, the pattern of the chemical molecules in the double helix did resemble a musical staff. By assigning a note to each chemical he was able to play tunes from the A-chain and B-chain insulin molecules, and tunes from various other configurations of DNA molecules (Osgood).

In his research, Dr. Susumu Ohno (Tokyo/USA) converted the chemical formulas into musical notes and found music resembling that of the baroque and romantic eras. Dr. Ohno concluded that this genetic influence explains the affinity of music in man and nature. He discovered that music from cancer-producing cells sounded somber and funeral-like, while music from the lens of an eye is "filled with trills and flourishes, airy, and light" (Humes: 8). We can then agree with David who said:

Psalm 139:13-17

"For thou hast possessed my reigns: thou hast covered me in my mother's womb. I will praise thee; for I am fearfully and wonderfully made: marvelous are thy works; and that my soul knoweth right well. My substance was not hid from thee, when I was made in secret, and curiously wrought in the lowest parts of the earth. Thine eyes did see my substance, yet being unperfect; and in thy book all my members were written which in continuance were fashioned, when as yet there was none of them. How precious are thy thoughts unto me, O God! how great is the sum of them!"

Music affects the human body in a variety of ways. Because the "roots of auditory nerves are more widely distributed and have more extensive connections than those of any other nerves in the body, most of our body functions are affected by the pulsations and the harmonic combination of musical tones" (Torres: 18). Sound waves (vibrations) and sympathetic vibrations acting upon the ear drum are transformed to chemical and nerve impulses which register in our minds the different timbres we hear. They give shocks in rhythmical sequence to muscles which causes them to contract and set in motion our arms, hands, legs, feet, and elicit physical responses such as sex, hunger, thirst, etc.

Since music directly attacks the nervous system and does not depend upon the master brain to gain entrance into the organism, the result is that, via the thalamus part of the brain lying below the main cerebellum, the seat of our emotions, sensations and feelings can be aroused. However, "the spoken word must pass through the master brain to be interpreted, translated, and screened for moral content. Therefore, the music that we hear affects the nervous system, the autonomic nervous system, and the whole body" (Larson: RR 68).

Music is an aspect of our physical environment that has an effect upon the health and well-being of the human body. Since the body is able to discriminate between beneficial and detrimental sounds, it constantly seeks to adjust to its environment by trying to put and keep things in order. When surrounded by "agreeable" sounds the body is invigorated, energized, and balanced (Diamond: 98).

There are twelve meridians (paths) related to specific body organs that affect the muscles: bladder, circulation, sex organs, gall bladder, heart, kidney, large and small intestines, liver, lung, spleen, stomach, and thyroid. Negative emotions that weaken the thymus gland are fear, hate, anger, etc. Since every major muscle of the body relates to an organ, this means that all organs in the body are affected by a large portion of the popular music to which it is exposed each day. The problem becomes quite serious in light of the many hours of radio play throughout the world (Diamond: 100).

The relationship between the thymus gland and agreeable music is very significant. This gland (prevalent in youth but disappears in adulthood) is the link between the mind and the body. It is a factory for producing lymphocytes which are responsible for the immunological reactions of the "T" cells. It controls, monitors, and regulates energy flow in the meridian system, and is the first organ in the body to be affected by one's physical environment, social relationships, food, posture, negative emotions, and stress (as is characteristic of rap and other popular music) (Diamond: 27-29).

Two thousand years ago, Plato, as did other Greeks, recognized the effect of music upon the human being and therefore demanded that strict censorship be placed over popular music in his Utopian Republic. He said that "the citizens would be tempted and corrupted by weak and voluptuous airs and led to indulge in demoralizing emotions" (Key: MS 118). Also aware of the tremendous influence of music upon the listener, Claudio Monteverdi, a late Renaissance composer, said that "the end of all good music is to affect the soul" (Larson: DMD 113). "If these scholars could recognize the powerful affect of music during their day, then we all must be prudent in our listening habits in order to avoid the moral destruction of our nation" (Larson: RR 72). From that time to the present, music has always reflected the changes and mores of society. And today, as the newspapers and other media are filled with reports of crime, violence, and economic and social problems, willing or not, ready or not, we are all involved.

When considering the characteristics of today's popular music, the *rock* element is the dominant characteristic that has the most adverse effect upon the human body. It consists of the loud volume and the driving beat (back beats that emphasize the weak beats, and the stopped anapestic beat). The old rock and roll beat of the 1950s does not seem to have this "*stopped*" quality. According to music critic Robert Palmer, "when rock and roll is really rocking and rolling, it combines an irresistible forward motion, a heavy back beat, and a certain lightness or lilt. . . ." (Diamond: 101).

The stopped anapestic beat weakens the body because it goes against the natural rhythm of human physiology, thus affecting the heart and blood pressure. The body tends to respond to the beat with muscle weakness, anxiety, aggressive behavior, and a craving for more. It sets in motion the autonomic fright-and-flight response, thus causing a secretion of the hormone, epinephrin (Diamond: 101). Since the sound and the message of this music communicate more than the words, the purpose of the sound is to consume the listener. The beat and volume were the identifying characteristics of the counterculture of the 1960s and the ensuing generations, thus signifying rebellion against parents and authority. Companions of the rock music were (and still are) drugs, immorality, rebellion, violence, etc.

Another negative physical effect of the rock beat is *switching*, a homolateral movement in the brain causing one-sided brain activity because the brain waves are out of sync. As a result, the body is in a state of confusion and alarm. Switching also causes perceptual difficulties, a decrease in performance (in school and work output), hyperactivity and restlessness, reduction in decision-making capacity, and a loss of energy for no apparent reason. There is also a drop in blood sugar (the brain's nutrition source) which, over a period of time, results in structural changes in the brain cells. This subsequently causes the body to be unable to distinguish between that which is good or that which is harmful. It also reverses the principles of morality and rejects the good and welcomes the bad (Diamond: 103).

Volume is another aspect of the negative impact that rock music has upon the body. It involves a set number of vibrations per cycle per second, and is measured in decibel units. A sound at 10 decibels equals 10 times the energy as a 0 decibel sound. A 20 decibel sound is 100 times the intensity of a 0 decibel sound. The threshold of feeling is 120 decibels. While one experiences pain at 140 decibels, prolonged volume over 85 decibels damages hearing. Rock concerts generally falls within the range of 120-160 decibels, 110-116 decibels for night clubs, and at about 110 decibels for religious concerts.

The intensity of the vibrations and the volume produces a loss of hearing, and an over-secretion of epinephrin which over stimulates the sex glands without a normal release (Larson: RR 81). On an ABC documentary, Prime Time, February 11, 1993, Dr. Helen Fischer, a pioneer in research for scientific reasons for why we do what we do when we are in love, stated that there are two stages of love. The first stage is that of infatuation. In this state the body produces amphetamines (dorphomine, norphonephrine, and phenalethelalmi-PEA) which causes giddiness, euphoria, hope, lust, apprehension and sleepiness. The second stage is that of romance or companionship. In this state the body produces endorphines that cause intense feelings of pleasure as is experienced from a morphine high, savoring sweet tasting food, or a runner's high; and like the drug addict, many depend upon music to get that same feeling. Other scientific studies have revealed that plants and mice incur inhibited growth when subjected to music containing the rock element. Some of the results were a loss of learning capacity because of unconnected neurons in the brain where they are controlled, and irreversible brain damage. Humans are affected the same way (Diamond: 103). In a music seminar back in the late 1960s Bob Larson, a former rock music musician, told how some of the musicians in his band would take raw eggs to rock concerts and place them near the amplifiers. By the end of the concert the eggs would be soft boiled. If this could happen to an egg, just imagine what happens to the brain when listening to such music.

The media has also capitalized upon the opportunity to use rock to subliminally seduce the public. Today we are being bombarded and negatively influenced through the senses by both the conscious and subliminal stimuli that we encounter each day. Subliminal seduction is the process of using audio or visual means to subconsciously manipulate one's behavior. "There are three main types of emotional experiences to which the subconscious is sensitive: 1) the *social* which is associated with cultural conflicts, taboos, i.e. morality, hair, dress, etc.; 2) or the *psychological* which deals with neurosis, psychosis, phobic responses, paranoia, etc.; 3) and the *physical* which is influential in triggering the memory by effecting drive-related behavior such as sex, aggression, hunger, thirst, etc. Subliminal stimuli have also been effective in activating the autonomic bodily functions such as blood pressure, pulse rate, and respiration" (Key: SS 34). TV commercials especially capitalize upon this in the promotion of sales.

Research on the phenomenon of subliminal perception has been conducted for centuries by scholars such as Democritus (400 B.C.), Plato, Aristotle, and even Sigmund Freud and his colleagues in the late 19th and 20th centuries. They all concluded that the many perceptions that go unnoticed or unremembered would one day become conscious consequences. Aristotle said that "the powerful impulses that occurred during the day would become noticeable during the time of sleep", and hence, "this would cause one to hear thunder and lightening when actually a faint noise had occurred. Freud and his colleagues concluded that subliminal stimuli can have a delayed reaction upon one's behavior and thus, "a conscious association can trigger a subliminal precept buried deeply in the unconscious mind weeks, months, or years after the subliminal perception occurred" (Key: SS 19).

The awareness of subliminal manipulation came to the attention of the public in the late 1950's when James Vicary, an American marketing researcher, demonstrated the effects of the tachistoscope, a machine used to flash subliminal messages on the movie screen and thereby manipulate the behavior of mass audiences. In spite of legislative attempts made to control this anomalous violation of one's freedom of choice, efforts were unsuccessful in prohibiting the use of subliminal techniques in public communication media. By the late 1960's subliminal perception had been extensively tested and overwhelmingly successful in influencing eight areas of human behavior—dreams, memory, value norm anchor points, conscious perceptions, verbal behavior, emotion, drives, and perception defenses (Key: SS 20).

Auditory perception at the conscious level is limited to a finite range of sound, volume, and tone frequency levels. Beyond these ranges are frequencies where information can be inaudibly transmitted into the unconscious. The silent dog whistle is an example of high pitched sound frequencies that are inaudible to the human conscious perception. Data transmitted at these high frequencies will be registered in the unconscious mind. Conversely, it is possible to introduce tones and harmonies at sub-audible levels in the bass range that can only be detected when the volume is increased. By increasing the volume of popular music, thereby selectively manipulating the value norm anchor points of loud and soft between the younger and older age group, rock music has become even more special to the youth culture (Key: SS 27).

Record producers, with their highly sophisticated electronic equipment, have begun to manipulate the thoughts and behavior of the youth culture by injecting subliminal messages into rock music which can only be heard at the conscious level by increasing the volume and expanding the frequency range. These messages are hidden in relatively simple verbal or musical illusions through the technique of metacontrast or backward masking. For example, the 1974 hit group, Blue Swede, "*Hooked On A Feeling,*" has a background chant "ooh-ga-shook-ah," which, to the conscious perception, makes little sense. It is when the attention is focused upon the foreground lyrics that at several intervals during the chant, the words are imperceptibly converted into "who got sucked off?" This technique is known as metacontrast or backward masking. When played backward, a Led Zippelin rock music tape, *"Stairway to Heaven,"* bore the consciously perceptible phrases "Here's to my sweet Satan," and "I live for Satan" (Key: MS 118).

Today, however, the value system was changed to appeal to the unconscious and seems to be related to Freud's theory of the "human death wish" or "death instinct." Death and self-destruction are successful subliminal merchandising techniques in alcohol, tobacco, drugs, and other such products. Authorities have even reported finding some meta-contrast phrases in suicide notes of young people.

The music market, like commercial researchers, have studied for years the cultural life styles, purchasing patterns, psychosexual development, mating customs, and the whole gamut of complex needs within individuals, and thus skillfully markets their products to specific groups and subgroups within society. The record industry is cognizant of the fact that young people have a natural tendency to identify with the music that has fast tempos and the driving rock beat in contrast to the music preferred by the older generation. They have even capitalized on the opportunity to make millions of dollars by fusing the current popular sounds with religious words.

It all began in 1969 with Edwin Hawkin's arrangement of *"Oh Happy Day."* Never before had a "religious" song been aired on a secular "Top 40" radio program, to say nothing of becoming a number one hit. Since that time many religious record companies have evolved and have not only begun to emulate the marketing techniques of secular record companies, but have become more sophisticated as well; not like the amateur style of past years. This trend led to the merger of religious music with the use of secular production and marketing techniques.

Subliminal manipulation of words and phrases in *crossover songs* create and influence romantic and/or sexual fantasies or any other type of thought manipulation. But even more subtle than that are the religious "pronoun" songs that allude to God without ever calling His name—*"He's Everything To Me"* or *"When I Get In His Presence."* There is much power in the name of Jesus. **GOD SAYS. . .**

Acts 4:12

"For there is none other name under heaven given among men, whereby we must be saved."

Ephesians 1:21

"Far above all principality, and power, and might, and dominion, and every name that is named, not only in the world, but also in that which is to come."

Philippians 2:10-11

"That at the name of Jesus every knee should bow, of things in heaven, and things in earth, and things under the earth; And that every tongue should confess that Jesus Christ is Lord, to the glory of God the Father."

The enemy is determined to do everything possible to prevent us from having anything to do with God, even calling His name in songs of praise. Many of these "pronoun" songs are really nice songs; we just have to be aware of what is happening in the lyrics and substitute the name of Jesus for some of these pronouns.

Not only have the recording industry and other media taken advantage of this tactic to make big bucks in sales, but so has the food industry. Did you know that music affects your diet? Marketing strategists know this and hence, target, program, and manipulate the purchasing and eating habits of consumers. This is why all the fast food commercials use up-tempo music to sell their products. In addition to this, when you go in to purchase your food and the music playing is fast you will purchase more and eat more. Research by Johns Hopkins University videoed eaters and found that without background music 3.9 bites were consumed per minute and it took about 40 minutes to eat. Only a third of this group requested seconds. When the music was fast 5.1 bites per minute were consumed within a thirty minute period and almost all returned for seconds. When slow music was played 3.2 bites were consumed per minute and this group took up to sixty minutes to eat. They even left food and said that the food had more taste when they chewed slower (Brick: AH 90).

Another piece to the rock music scenario is that of Sentics, the science of emotional communication. This reveals how emotions are communicated in daily life through music and the arts. This emotional communication transcends cultural lines because there is something intrinsic in how music is put together. This is one reason why music is considered to be the universal language. The musical elements that create images or *sound forms* of emotion are pitch, intensity, timbre, duration, and harmonic progression.

The essetic forms of human emotions are love, joy, anger, hate, grief, sex, reverence, etc. Due to their cyclic nature, they are not interchangeable nor can they be expressed simultaneously. For example, the cycle for the emotion of reverence is 9.8 seconds, joy is 5.2 seconds, grief is 8.2 seconds, love is 7.4 seconds, sex is 4.9 seconds, and anger, 4.2 seconds. Therefore, the emotions of joy and anger or reverence and joy cannot be expressed simultaneously because their cycles do not coincide. Scientifically, this is why funeral music is slow, and music that is happy and joyful is faster (Clynes: S 41).

Today's trends in popular music, however, replace sentics with sound sensory environments and reactions and responses which seek to bombard one with "effects" instead of appealing to reason and understanding. Since music is an expression of the soul, that which one feeds upon will influence the character, for by beholding one becomes changed. While the youth act out the lyrics of today's popular music, society is subjected to, and is experiencing their rebellion, their hot-tempered and aggressive personalities, the glorification of immorality and trash, questionable and/or indecent fashion, and the polarization of youth and age.

It is imperative then that we, as musicians, educators, and Christians develop a strategy and begin a campaign to reverse what is happening to society through our youth, and counteract the negative results with positive experiences through music programs in our schools and churches that will teach principles that will enhance intellectual and spiritual growth and development. These programs are needed to make the youth aware of the adverse effects of today's popular music upon the mind, body, and soul, and teach them how to choose suitable music that will have a refining influence upon the character.

Summary

While out walking on a certain crisp fall morning, it was still warm enough for me to hear the crickets chirping their song of praise to the

Creator. As I began to focus upon other sounds, I realized just how much our lives are governed by sound. From the time we awake until the time we fall asleep, and even throughout the night, we are exposed to hundreds of sounds—the infamous alarm clock awaking us from a pleasant slumber; the birds singing; the heating/AC unit; the hum in the flourescent lights; and the list goes on. Within a split second four steps take place in the hearing process—the ear hears the sound produced; the brain registers the sound; a mental image is formed; and we respond physically or emotionally, or both.

Through conditioning, sounds that were once offensive can eventually become tolerable. This is especially true with music. I remember when songs like *"Pass It On"* and *"He's Everything to Me"* were considered to be too "up beat" and objectionable. Compared to today's music, they are like pabulum. Conditioning involves building up a tolerance for something; changing or conforming. As was discussed earlier in the chapter, the media is the primary source of such conditioning. We hear pop music when we listen to the news or commercials; in grocery stores and shopping malls; coming from someone else's car while in traffic; in other words, it is omnipresent. Thus, we have become conditioned to it.

Another fact to consider is that music can either be *programatic*—designed to subliminally effect imaginative suggestions, or it can be *absolute (neutral)*—void of any subliminal or extra musical effects that provoke imaginative suggestions. Because of this, choices and value judgments should be made according to the message that the music conveys because it speaks much louder than words. Since it is an expression of the soul, then what one consistently consumes will have an impact upon the character; "the harvest is of the same nature as the seed sown" (White: 6T 194). In light of this, how can we not be affected by what we listen to? The difference lies in whether or not we "hear" it or "listen" to it.

Barring any physical disabilities, hearing is a natural response to sounds over which we have no control; we hear what we hear. Listening, however, is a choice. It involves opening up the mind and subjecting it to what we hear. We concentrate, pay thoughtful attention, form mental images, and subdue other senses when we listen. In other words, we permanently record in our minds what we listen to.

There is an axiom that says "garbage in—garbage out." We are that which we feed upon. If strength of body, mind, and character are the desired result, then diligent effort must be put forth to achieve that goal. Even if only from a secular perspective, the scientific facts listed above substantiate the importance of choosing suitable music for optimum physical, mental, and spiritual health. "All should guard the senses, lest Satan gain victory over them, for these are the avenues of the soul" (White: AH 402).

CHAPTER THIRTEEN

SECULAR MUSIC

Not long ago I was listening to one of Paul Harvey's news broadcasts and heard him tell about a recent experiment whereby mice were timed to see how long it would take them to go through a maze. On the first round they went through without any music five minutes faster than the control group. The second time around classical music was played and they went through eight minutes faster. The third time "pop music" was played and not only did it take them twenty minutes longer, but they turned on one another and began killing themselves. If music can have that much of an effect on mice, then the same is true for humans. Their behavior is a graphic reflection of the condition of our society today. The music we choose is just as important to our spiritual health as eating is to our physical health, whether it is sacred or secular.

Although the purpose of this book is to address issues pertaining to church music, I will, however, say a word about secular music, jazz in particular. For practical reasons, I will address this issue only as it pertains to those previously discussed to see if the "myths" about it are substantial, for, believe it or not, I frequently hear it performed in many churches, and all the people say "amen." I observed a long time ago that jazz is accepted as church music if it is not labeled or perceived as such. But the question still remains, if jazz is inappropriate music then why is it permitted to be performed in church?

Jazz, like the spiritual, is a musical development that grew to become an authentic American art form. Initially, it evolved as a fusion of blues, ragtime, brass bands, and dance rhythms influenced by European and African traditions. Being vocally oriented, it contained some of the very same characteristics as the spiritual, the only difference being that players replaced the voice with instruments, thus imitating the characteristic style of singing—blues notes, sliding, bending, surging, in addition to rich harmonies, rhythm, syncopation, improvisation, and ornamentation, etc. (See Southern, 361) It is considered by some to be the counterpart of European classical music—the black man's version. Today there exist many different types—avant-garde, bebop, big band, boogie-woogie, classical jazz, cool jazz, Dixieland, jazz rock/fusion, jazz /rock/pop fusion, gospel jazz, and the list goes on. In light of this, it is evident that jazz cannot and should not be categorized as one style of music because there are many, and, like classical music, it can also be divided into different eras. Let's take a brief walk through the annals of history to ascertain its origin.

By the time the United States purchased Louisiana in 1803, New Orleans, a multi-cultural center, had been under the rule of two flags— the Spanish and the French—and each left its influence upon the evolution of jazz. In France the military band reached its peak under Napoleon, and in New Orleans the colony of French settlers continued this tradition (Sousa style). Before the Civil War these bands consisted of whites, creoles (offspring from intermarriages between the Spanish, French, and Africans), and free blacks who had the privilege of acquiring musical training; some were even educated in France. As a result, the European tradition became the predominant influence, thus overshadowing African traditions.

After the Civil War many of these bands dissolved and the instruments were either discarded or pawned. Former slaves now had access to the abandoned instruments and formed their own street bands. As southern whites migrated to New Orleans with their ideas on race and color, creoles and former slaves from other locations who also migrated there got caught in the middle of segregation. At first fair skinned creoles didn't participate in the musical practices of "uptown" blacks, but tried to maintain the European style of music. However, as prejudice grew, all creoles had to move "uptown" with their counterparts after the city enacted a segregation code in 1894. With the merger of the European (musical notation) and African (aural) traditions, bands began to emerge and functioned for almost all occasions—picnics, parades, funerals, river boat excursions, concerts, and dancing, which became the rage (during Ellen White's day). Famous bands like the Charles "Buddy" Bolden band set the style for New Orleans jazz and instrumentation which included the cornet, clarinet, trombone, bass, banjo or guitar, and drums. It is said that he is the first known jazz band leader, and that he got his ideas for jazz when he went to *church* each week (Megill: 20). As a result, many dance halls sprang up. One of the main patrons of this new music was Storyville (named after Alderman Sidney Story who instituted a resolution for "vice segregation"), an entertainment district in New Orleans (See Southern: 341). It is because of this association that jazz earned a bad reputation.

There are two theories regarding the origin of the name, jazz. The first says that it was named after an itinerant musician named Jazbo Brown who was well known in the Mississippi Valley. It is alleged that when he played in the bars the patrons would shout "More, Jazbo! More, Jaz, more!" The second theory is that around 1910 in Chicago, Boisey James painted signs for musicians which said "Music will be furnished by Jas' Band." Because of his fondness for this music he became known as "Old Jas", and the music he played, referred to as "Jas's music.", and finally "jazz" (Southern: 361).

Jazz, like other musical forms, is not static; it continuously changes and is interwoven into the fabric of social development, adopting and incorporating various idioms and expressions that make it appealing to both old and young. Even classical composers like Maurice Ravel, Igor Stravinsky, Darius Milhaud, and George Gershwin incorporated jazz idioms into their music (Broekema: 232). Nowadays, jazz is no longer relegated to one particular culture or ethnic group. As a matter of fact, in the music world there exists a controversy regarding whether or not any one culture can claim jazz as its own creation; whether or not it can be stolen; or whether or not it can be changed at will (See Megill: 7). What has actually happened is that over a period of time concomitant styles and idioms have been combined, thus changing its meaning and "ownership," and making it the melting pot of musical expression for diverse cultures.

Whenever I am asked whether or not jazz is "ok" to listen to, I believe that the real issue is whether or not it is ok to listen to *secular* music. All things considered, its origin and development make it the counterpart of "pop rock". The style characteristics and metamorphosis do not change the fact that jazz is secular music and therefore should not be separated or singled out as something different. This fact is often overlooked or misunderstood, and as a result, has caused jazz to fall victim to condemnation. Just as there is "good" and "bad" religious music, "good" and "bad" classical music, there is also "good and "bad" secular music, each of which expresses human emotions and sentiments.

Music serves a functional purpose within our lives. We listen to it to express personal feelings, to enrich us, to entertain us, to provide background "noise" while dining or doing other things, to set a romantic atmosphere, to worship God, etc. Because we spend the majority of our time involved in secular activities, it stands to reason that there will be secular music to coincide with some of these activities. There are even citations in Holy Writ that refer to the use of secular music: farewell parties (Genesis 31:27); a joyous homecoming (Judges 11:34); work songs (Numbers 21:17, 18), etc. It is most interesting to note that some Bible scholars consider the victory songs of Miriam and Deborah to be secular (Achetemeier: 667).

Ellen White (see Preface) enjoyed a variety of music, secular included. She "did not condemn it just because it might be secular." (Hamel: 64) She even wrote about some of the concerts that she attended and really enjoyed. Once, while sailing to Europe, the ship was delayed so the musicians on board gave a concert. She said that " the musicians who were to leave the boat at this place entertained the impatient passengers with music, well selected and well rendered. It did not jar upon the senses as the previous evening, but was soft and really grateful to the senses because it was musical" (White Letter, 6b). While in Europe she attended a concert in a public park and said that "there was beautiful music and fireworks close by across the road. There is an extensive beergarden owned by the city and carried on by the city. This garden is made attractive with flowers and shrubs and noble trees, giving a nice shade. There are seats that will accommodate hundreds, and little oval tables are adjusted before these seats and this most beautiful instrumental music is played by the band" (White Manuscript).

Even Jesus, while on this earth, had a secular side to His life and therefore engaged in secular activities—His job as a carpenter; attending the wedding feast in which he turned the water into wine; cooking breakfast for the disciples who had been out all night fishing, etc. If secular music is indeed inappropriate for Christians as some conscientiously believe it is, then what is to be the substitute for those events that call for secular music—wedding receptions (not weddings), banquets, socials, patriotic events, and the like; What is to become of the highly esteemed classical music, much of which is secular? If it has moral and ethical value, what is wrong with it? Songs such as *"I Believe I Can Fly," "We Are The World," That's What Friends Are For,"* or *"You'll Never Walk Alone"* all have moral and ethical value that will entertain, ennoble, and edify the listener although they are secular. The only danger of secular music, however, is that of intemperate consumption which can subtly turn one's attention away from spiritual things. It is imperative to set limits upon the amount of time that is spent listening to secular music.

God has given every human being the power of choice even when it comes to music. However, with this privilege comes the responsibility of being careful not to offend the "weaker" brother or sister who may be trying to "overcome." I would caution that extremes should be avoided because they are counterproductive. To be so heavenly minded that one is of no earthly good is just as bad as the reverse; both bring reproach upon Christianity. The key to avoiding this predicament is *balance* and *variety*. Knowing and understanding that we must deal with this issue, **GOD SAYS. . .**

Luke 20:25

> *"Render therefore unto Caesar the things which be Caesar's, and unto God the things which be God's."*

Romans 14:5,13-22

> *"Let every man be fully persuaded in his own mind. . . That no man put a stumbling block or an occasion to fall in his brother's way. . . But if thy brother be grieved. . . now walkest thou not charitably. Destroy not him. . . for whom Christ died. Let not your good be evil spoken of. . . Let us therefore*

follow after the things which make for peace, and things wherewith one may edify another. Destroy not the work of God. All things indeed are pure; but it is evil for that man who eateth with offence. It is good [to do] any thing whereby thy brother stumbleth, or is offended, or is made weak. . . ."

1 Corinthians 8:9

"But take heed lest by any means this liberty of yours become a stumbling block to them that are weak."

1 Corinthians 13:5

"Charity. . . seeketh not her own. . . ."

Galatians 5:22, 23

"But the fruit of the Spirit is. . . temperance: against such there is no law."

Summary

Music has many functions besides being a medium through which feelings, ideas, emotions, and moods can be expressed. Because Christians have a secular side to life, it is reasonable to assume that "good" secular music exists to correspond with like activities. However, as I pointed out earlier in the chapter, a steady diet of secular music will, without question, stunt or even kill one's spirituality. Conversely, believe it or not, there looms the danger of sacred music achieving the same result when used inappropriately. One of the most subtle deceptions of the enemy is that of deluding well-meaning Christians into believing that one should only consume sacred music. The motive is noble, but the philosophy borders upon fanaticism which can lead to the desecration of scared music. For example, when used for secular purposes it becomes trivial and common, thus losing its effectiveness in being a channel through which the Holy Spirit can speak to the heart. The mind becomes conditioned to its indiscriminate usage and will eventually dismiss it as being sacred—something special and "holy." It soon has the effect of a dripping faucet to which one turns a deaf ear. This is just as Satan would have it. The key to avoiding this situation is to be practical and *avoid extremes,* understanding that music is *functional* and should be *appropriate for the occasion.* Balance and variety should exist between the sacred and the secular. After all, we are admonished to be temperate in all things.

CHAPTER FOURTEEN

PRINCIPLES, STANDARDS, AND GUIDELINES OF "GOOD" MUSIC

God's character, represented by the Ten Commandments, is under attack, and music is one of the tools used to effect this malignity. Our participation in this heinous crime can, however, be avoided by discovering God's word on how to handle this challenge, understanding the purpose of music, and realizing that the enemy of our souls is the source of the problem. Some of his fiendish methods involve mixing the holy with the profane and getting us caught up in worldliness. He creates confusion on issues about worship, music ministry, singing in worship, instruments in worship, and the "holy" dance (not condoned by the church system). The effect of music upon the mind and the body, including secular music, plays a vital role in this warfare. In light of this, the following principles, standards, and guidelines are designed to identify and reflect who we are and whose we are as a church body, to corroborate this identity in a way that will be edifying, enriching, ennobling, and enjoyable to the individual, and to establish a means of implementation in order to provide balance and variety; after all, that is God's way of doing things.

PRINCIPLES

Music is one of God's entrusted talents. It is a powerful tool that can be used to uplift, edify, inspire, elevate, evangelize, reinforce doctrine and beliefs, "subdue rude and uncultivated natures," and promote harmony of action. It can fix words in the memory and impress the heart with spiritual truth, serve as a weapon against discouragement, and "bring heaven's gladness to the soul."It also serves as a means of employment, as well as "re-creation" (leisure activities that have redemptive qualities). Therefore, music should be rendered with "dignity manifested by discipline, with solemnity and awe, with clear intonation, and with distinct utterance" at a volume that will not be overpowering or jarring to the senses (See Task Force on the Philosophy of Music). In light of these qualities, the church believes that:

1) All music should build and have a refining influence upon the character. *"But the fruit of the Spirit is love, joy, peace, longsuffering, gentleness, goodness, faith, meekness, temperance: against such there is no law"* (Galatians 5:22-23).

"The religion of Christ will refine the taste, sanctify the judgment, elevate, purify, and ennoble the soul, making the Christian more and more fit for the society of the heavenly angels" (White: TKH 250).

2) Music should be appropriate to perform or listen to in the presence of God. *"Whither shall I go from thy spirit? Or whither shall I flee from thy presence? If I ascend up into the heaven, thou art there: if I make my bed in hell, behold, thou art there. If I take the wings of the morning, and dwell in the uttermost parts of the sea; even there shall thy hand lead me. . ."* (Psalm 139:7-10).

"In every place, at every hour in the day, there is a holy Watcher who balances every account, whose eye takes in the whole situation, whether it is one of fidelity or one of disloyalty and deception. We are never alone. We have a companion whether we choose Him or not.

Remember, young men and young women, that wherever you are, whatever you are doing, [whatever you are listening to], God is there. To your every word and action you have a witness— the holy, sin-hating God. Nothing that is said or done or thought can escape His infinite eye. . . . In the deepest darkness and solitude He is there. . . . None can escape from their accountability to Him" (White: TMK 234).

3) Music should have moral and ethical value in order to promote spiritual and intellectual growth. ". . .*Grow up into Him in all things, which is the head, even Christ: From whom the whole body fitly joined together and compacted by that which every joint supplieth, according to the effectual working in the measure of every part, maketh increase of the body unto the edifying of itself in love*" (Ephesians 5:15-16).

"Where there is spiritual health there is growth. The child of God grows up to the full stature of a man or woman in Christ. There is no limit to his improvement" (White: 5T 265).

Hymns represent the music of the corporate body. They incorporate and reinforce the doctrines and philosophy of the church and function as a vehicle through which the Holy Spirit can speak to the heart. A consistent musical diet of non-liturgical, contemporary, and animated "praise" music in lieu of hymns will spiritually weaken the congregation and render them deficient in a knowledge of who they are and whose they are.

4) Music is either sacred or secular; the holy should not be mixed with the profane. ". . .*Teach my people the difference between the holy and profane, and cause them to discern between the unclean and the clean*" (Ezekiel 44:23).

There is no such thing as "*gospel jazz*" or "*Christian Rap*," etc. This is an oxymoron. The gospel is the good news of salvation—that Jesus suffered inhumane abuse in order to save us. To trivialize the gospel by mixing it with that which is secular (commercial) is not only sacrilegious, but is an affront of the greatest magnitude toward Jesus Christ. Rap "*music*" is rhythmic *speech* which contradicts the biblical directive to "sing" and make "melody." The enemy does not want us to "sing unto the Lord," so he created a counterfeit for singing. Unfortunately, there are those who have deluded themselves into believing that such music can be used to lead others to Christ. God never has nor will He ever use the devil's tools to attract sinners unto Himself.

"There is always danger, when the common is mingled with the sacred, that the common will be allowed to take the place of the sacred. . . When objectionable matter is mingled with sacred matter. . .[God's] blessing cannot rest upon the work done" (White: 8T 88).

5) Music should be *"functional"*—appropriate for the occasion. *"TO EVERY thing there is a season, and a time to every purpose under the heaven"* (Ecclesiastes 3:1).

Appropriate music is that which is acceptable, agreeable, apropos, becoming, befitting, compatible, complementary, correct, decent, exemplary, expedient, fitting, modest, pertinent, presentable, proper, relevant, and seemly, and the list goes on. Whatever the occasion, the music should fit the event. Other factors that must be considered are the context, the environment, the association, and the occasion. For example, although *"Let Us Break Their Bonds Asunder"* from <u>Messiah</u>, or "It Is Well With My Soul" are wonderful pieces, it would be inappropriate to hear them performed at a wedding which, by the way, is a *sacred* service. Secular love songs such as "You Are So Beautiful to Me", or "Sunrise, Sunset" (which are, in general, "good" songs) are inappropriate for a sacred service. Conversely, it would be inappropriate to use *"You Light Up My Life"* in worship (a "pronoun song") because it is not a religious song nor was it ever intended to be. A good rule to follow is "when in doubt, don't," especially if it is commercial in sound.

6) Music should not be harmful to the body temple. *"What? Know ye not that your body is the temple of the Holy Ghost which is in you, which ye have of God, and ye are not your own? For ye are bought with a price: therefore glorify God in your body, and in your spirit, which are God's. If any man defile the temple of God, him shall God destroy; for the temple of God is holy, which temple ye are"* (1 Corinthians 6:19,20; 3:17).

". . .Every action of the human agent should be in perfect harmony with the laws of life. . . Men and women should be informed in regard to the human habitation, fitted up by our Creator as His dwelling place, and over which He desires us to be faithful stewards" (White: 7T 136).

"For every offense committed against the laws of health, the transgressor must pay the penalty in his own body" (White: 4T 409).

By exciting the body and paralyzing the thoughts, the enemy uses certain elements of music (beat, vibrations, volume, tempo, and even instrumentation) in order to take possession of our minds. When God permitted Satan to test Job, from that day to this, he has afflicted the human body in an effort to make us "curse God [through our words, actions, and behavior] and die."

You have just read about some of the scientist research describing the profound effect that music has upon the body—hearing loss, jarred senses, sensory overload, increased blood pressure and heart rate, excess hormone secretion, perceptual difficulties, confusion, hyperactivity, restlessness, inhibited growth, a loss of learning capacity, decreased blood sugar (the brain's source of nutrition), structural changes in brain cells, irreversible brain damage. These maladies, in addition to others, are a direct result of the physical abuse that music can inflict upon the body.

Another interesting point to ponder is the fact that the body was constructed to move forward. These musical elements offset involuntary muscular contractions that set our bodies in motion, causing them to sway from side to side or convulse (often interpreted as a response to the Holy Spirit). This is a visible manifestation of the SOS that the body is sending. How can the Holy Spirit comfortably reside in such an environment?

7) Music should have artistic qualities ("beauty, pathos, and power") that can stand the test of time—not be a fad that will soon pass away. *"For all that is in the world, the lust of the flesh, and the lust of the eyes, and the pride of life, is not of the Father, but is of the world. And the world passeth away and the lust thereof. . ."* (1 John 2:16,17).

"We are living in a time when everything that is false and superficial is exalted above the real, the natural, and the enduring. The mind must be kept free from everything that would lead it in a wrong direction. It should not be encumbered with. . . [that] which does not add strength to the mental powers. The thoughts will be of the same character as the food we provide for the mind. . . When a wrong impression is made upon the mind in youth, a mark is made, not on sand, but on enduring rock" (White: 5T 544, 545).

8) Music should be edifying to the listener. *"Finally, brethren, whatsoever things are true, whatsoever things are honest, whatsoever things are just, whatsoever things are pure, whatsoever things are lovely, whatsoever things are of good report; if there be any virtue, and if there be any praise, thing on these things"* (Philippians 4:8).

"Frivolous songs and the popular sheet music of the day seem congenial to [the] taste. The instruments of music [tape recorders, CDs, videos, etc.] have taken time which should have been devoted to prayer. Music, when not abused, is a great blessing; but when put to a wrong use, it is a terrible curse. It excites, but does not impart that strength and courage which the Christian can find only at the throne of grace. . . to be fortified against the powerful temptations of the evil one. Satan is leading the young captive. . . I saw that Satan had blinded the minds of the youth that they could not comprehend the truths of God's word. Their sensibilities are so blunted that they regard not the injunctions of the holy apostle" (White: 1T 497).

9) Musical choices should not be offensive nor a stumbling block to anyone. *"All things are lawful for me, but all things are not expedient: all things are lawful for me, but all things edify not. Let no man seek his own, but every man another's wealth. . .whether therefore ye eat, or drink, or whatsoever ye do, do all to the glory of God. Give none offence, neither to the Jews, nor to the Gentiles, nor to the church of God: Even as I please all men in all things, not seeking mine own profit, but the profit of many, that they may be saved"* (1 Corinthians 10:23, 24; 31-33).

These texts are self-explanatory. Although we may have certain musical preferences, our choices should not be a stumbling block to one who is weak nor should they offend the church. God will hold us responsible for anyone who may be led astray because of our actions.

10) Musical choices should be made through the guidance of the Holy Spirit. *". . .The Spirit. . .will guide you into all truth. . ."* (John 16:13).

STANDARDS

The standards of music—*education, excellence, eternity*, and *service* (based upon attributes of truth, honesty, ethics, purity, aesthetics, philosophy (good report), virtue, and praise, as found in Philippians 4:8)—also reflect who we are and whose we are. They transcend moral issues of right and wrong to become spiritual issues engendering spiritual *consequences*.

1) Education is the vehicle that transports one from darkness into light. It is a key element in resolving many of these confusing and controversial issues about music. God does not want us to be in the dark about music; He wants us to have wisdom, knowledge, and understanding. *"The wisdom [about music] that comes from heaven is first of all pure; then*

peace-loving, considerate, submissive, full of mercy and good fruit, impartial and sincere" (James 3:17, NIV). Therefore, He has given us His word as *"a lamp unto [our] feet, and a light unto [our] path"* (Psalm 119:105). God advises that *"Wisdom is the principal thing; therefore get wisdom: and with all thy getting get understanding"* (Proverbs 4:7).

If one has been entrusted with musical talents and gifts, then one is under obligation to God to develop those talent to the fullest, whether or not for parochial or occupational reasons. This means obtaining a knowledge and understanding of the *discipline* of music—how to read music, how to sing properly, how to play instruments used in worship, how to direct a choir, etc. Not knowing can bring just as much of a reproach upon the cause of God as does knowing and not doing. The adversary will capitalize upon every opportunity to "make music a snare by the way in which it is conducted" (White: 1SM, p.37). God warns that we will be *"destroyed for lack of knowledge. . ."* (Hosea 4:6).

Since this church system does not employ ministers of music, individual churches are encouraged to provide continuing education for its musicians via workshops, mentoring, sponsorships, etc.

2) Excellence in music implies quality, expertise, accuracy, and preparation. If one were to be afforded the opportunity to perform for the President of the United States or some other dignitary, hours would be spent preparing for the occasion. Yet, this is not always the case when it comes to preparing for the work of the house of the Lord. Should God, the Giver of talents, be treated with any less respect? Just as there is "a lot of religion in a loaf of bread," there is a lot of religion in performing music well. The admonition *"Whatsoever thy hand findeth to do, do it with thy might"* (Ecclesiastes 9:10), and *"Whatsoever ye do, do all to the glory of God"* (1 Corinthians 10:31) leaves us without excuse. For a musician to ask the congregation for prayer before rendering music because of insufficient preparation or to have to apologize for blundering through a performance brings dishonor to God.

Another part of excellence acknowledges the fact that not everyone has been given gifts or talents in music. Therefore, God does not expect nor will He require an account of those to whom He has given no musical talent. He is not honored nor glorified by cacophonous attempts to produce music "in His name." Conversely, as in the parable of the talents, God is neither honored nor glorified by those who fail to *develop* their skills and abilities.

3) Eternity represents the motive for why we do what we do, and the goal which we are all striving to reach. We are admonished to "set [our] affection on things above, not on things on the earth" (Colossians 3:2). God's music has no resemblance whatsoever to that of the enemy. If our sacred music represents or reflects the commercial attributes of the music industry (the beat, the volume, sensuality, etc.) to the point that it can only be distinguished by the lyrics, then it does not represent our eternal destination, for the music of heaven is at enmity with that of the world. I often observe talented young people pursuing recording contracts for performing opportunities, fully intending to be a "witness" for God, yet not fully comprehending that good intentions often succumb to compromise. It is very difficult to focus on eternal things under these circumstances.

4) Service is the byword of Christianity. It means that the musical gifts and talents with which we have been endowed will be used to minister or lead others to Christ, whether parochially or occupationally. "We are most useful to God when we are most useful to others" (DeHann).

GUIDELINES

Although individuals make up the church body, the diversity of background, culture, geographic location, influence of society, and other variables render it impossible and impractical to cater to individual tastes and preferences without causing confusion. The church then must function as the spiritual leader and governing body in order to promote harmony of action in procedure, ministry, performance, and decorum among the collective body. "The church is bigger than any individual, its ministry far more important than our personal rights and desires! If we would only ask, 'How would my action affect the church and the program of Christ?' Instead, we insisted on our rights and hold to our position, even though it splits the church, ruins our testimony, and stops progress. . . [It is about] not seeking our own comfort and safety, but living for the good of the body of Christ" (DeHann)!

The following guidelines were formulated to articulate perimeters that coincide with the above philosophy and standards of music:

1) If the music does not ascribe to the doctrines and philosophy of the church, it is inappropriate.

2) If church musicians do not have communion with God on a daily basis, then they cannot effectively minister to the church in a way that nurtures, edifies, and speaks to the heart and conscious because they are not connected.

3) If the music is neither functional nor appropriate for the occasion, then it cannot effectively nurture and edify the collective body. If every assembly is treated as worship, then the spiritual and social needs of the congregation cannot be met—Bible study (Sabbath School), testimonies and prayer (Prayer Meeting), discussions and presentations (AY), outreach (Community Service and other support groups), "re-creation" (concerts, social events), business (Board, Church, and other departmental meetings, etc.)

4) If music does not engender reverence (respect) for God and His house of worship, then it is inappropriate.

5) If repetitious outbursts of praise cliches become an annoyance or distraction to anyone in the congregation, then it ceases to be edifying and thus becomes false worship (See Acts 16:16-18).

6) If behavioral responses of a congregation are orchestrated ("sit back and relax", "put your hands together", "say amen") or if a performer is being cheered while approaching the platform to render music, then a theatrical atmosphere is created because the focus of attention is directed to the performer.

7) If music for worship consists primarily of non-liturgical "religious" music or animated praise music, then it will not nurture the church and will eventually render the church spiritually weak and deficient in a knowledge of who we are and whose we are.

8) If the motive for choosing music for worship is rooted in culture and tradition, then it is directed toward the creature and not the Creator. "Tradition, without purpose, merely propagates more tradition, without fostering growth and forward thinking" (Ralph Neighbor, Jr.).

9) If music is poorly rendered, then it will not be an effective witness, nor will it be edifying to the congregation.

10) If the spirit, character, and manner in which music is rendered is associated with an environment that does not represent the church (night club, disco, etc.), then it is inappropriate.

11) If "church" music sounds like R&B, Rock, Rap, Jazz, Fusion, Country-Western, and other such secular "pop"genres, then it is inappro-

priate.

12) If a musical rendition is inundated with sensual overtones (guttural crooning, heavy breathing, etc.), then it is inappropriate.

13) If music is rendered in a sensational manner (vocal gymnastics, excessive use of ornamentation, keyboard runs, lavish chords, etc.) that dazzles, excites, or induces undulation, hand clapping, swaying, etc.), or if a musician elicits these and other responses from the congregation in an effort to "liven things up", then it is inappropriate. This "strange fire" undermines the work of the Holy Spirit because it does not come from the heart; it only honors the performer. Although a concert is the appropriate setting in which one's talent(s) can be displayed, all performances should be done "to the glory of God."

14) If musicians are competitive in spirit and unteachable, then their ministry will be tainted with selfishness, and thus, spiritually ineffective.

15) If a congregation cannot actively participate in worship because of the number of individual and group selections, then the occasion will become, by default, a spectator sport.

16) If the music or the musician becomes the "cherished idol" that absorbs the mind and diverts it from God, then they both will lose their effectiveness as vehicles for ministry.

17) If drums are used, then the musician should have a knowledge and understanding of their nature and function in music, and how they should be orchestrated—serving as a *"background"* instrument that adds "color" to music (cadence, climaxes), not loud and overpowering; not played throughout an entire piece; not played during prayer, responses, or at any other sensitive time within the service; not played during every hymn or musical selection; not changing the meaning or detracting from the message of the music by inducing undulating or any other physical response. This also includes sound tracks. Many are offended at the sight of drums within the sanctuary. Yet, what is the difference between a visible drummer and an invisible drummer (sound tracks, drum machine)? When improperly played the result is the same.

18) If any instrument (including sound tracks) overpowers the melody, harmony, and lyrics, then the music will only appeal to, and excite the senses, not the mind, for the message is lost.

19) If background music is used during the service, then it should be played very softly on only one instrument (not both piano and organ or

keyboards, etc.) so as not to distract the congregation or interfere with hearing what is being said. Background music can be very disturbing to persons with hearing disabilities, for they often cannot hear above the music.

20) If a musician "imitates" another artist or performs in a style that is not appropriate for the voice type, skill level, or ability, then the rendition will sound artificial and may not be edifying.

21) If secular music has moral value (elevating the thoughts to that which is pure, noble, virtuous, true, honest, and ethical), then it is appropriate for the collective body within context.

SUMMARY

Music is God's gift to humankind. It was given to us not only for His glory but for our enjoyment as well. Like a living organism it changes with time, and just like other elements of nature, it is subject to laws that govern the universe. It reflects the attitudes and mores of society and the myriad subcultures. Paradoxically, it is a wonderful servant and a hard master.

Music plays a functional role within our lives today just as it did for those living during Antiquity. Individual tastes and choices are often made because of the meaning that it has for the listener; because it touches that sensitive chord within; or because of how it makes the listener feel. As the end of time draws near, the enemy of our souls is using this most powerful tool to blur our spiritual vision and confuse our thinking, and as a result, many sincere persons are at a loss as to what is "right." For the individual, reliance upon the guidance of the Holy Spirit is crucial because all choices will, in the end, play a vital role in one's eternal destiny.

The church, on the other hand, bears the responsibility of spiritual leadership in the above issues on music. Its doctrines and philosophy are designed to govern the collective body and lead individuals into a closer relationship with God. The standards of education, excellence, eternity, and service represent the attributes of Christianity in the lifestyle, while the guidelines attempt to steer the collective body in the same direction.

Thus, you have read about the role that music will play in the new world order, its profound effect upon the mind, body, and character, and the spiritual consequences of choice. *"And the times of this ignorance God winked at; but now commandeth all men everywhere to repent: Because he hath appointed a day, in the which he will judge the world in righteousness. . ."* (Acts 17:30, 31).

"Let us hear the conclusion of the whole matter: Fear God, and keep his commandments for this is the whole duty of man" (Ecclesiastes 12:13).

Works Cited

Achtemeier, Paul J., et al. Harper's Bible Dictionary. 1985 ed.

Adler, Samuel. The Study of Orchestration. New York: Norton, 1982.

The Bible. King James Version.

Borekema, Andrew J. The Music Listener. Dubuque: Brown, 1982.

Brick, Pam. "Eat to the Beat: The Quicker the Tune the More You Consume." American
Health, vol 10. Jan. - Feb., 1991.

Clynes, Manfred. Sentics: The Touch of the Emotions. New York: Avery, 1989.

Dehann, Richard M. Our Dailey Bread. Grand Rapids: RBC Ministries, 1998.

Diamond, John. Behavioral Kinesiology. New York: Harper, 1979.

Hamel, Paul. Ellen White and Music. Washington D.C.: Review, 1976.

Harrington, Richard. "Christian Music Has Big Business Message." Huntsville Times. 10
Dec., 1980: 1C.

Horn, Siegfried H. ed. Seventh-day Adventist Bible Dictionary. 8 vols. Washington, DC:
Review, 1979.

Humes, Edward. "Scientist Hopes to Learn the Score Through Genetic Musical Compositions." (Santa Ana, California) Orange County Register, 4 Jan.1988: 8:F7.

Johnson, James Weldon, and Rosamand Johnson. "Lift Every Voice and Sing."

Jones, Claire. Making Music: Musical Instruments in Zimbabwe Past and Present. Zimbabwe: Academic, 1992.

Key, Wilson Bryan. Media Sexploitation. New York: NAL, 1976.

---. Subliminal Seduction. New York: NAL, 1973.

Larson, Bob. The Day Music Died. Carol Stream: Creation, 1972.

---. Rock & Roll: The Devils Diversion. McCook: Creation, 1970.

Martin, Malachi,. Keys of This Blood. New York: Simon, 1991.

Megill, David W., and Paul O.W. Tanner. Jazz Issues. Madison: Brown, 1995.

Osbeck, Kenneth W. Pocket Guide for the Church Choir Member. Grand Rapids: Kregal,

1985.

Osgood, Charles. "Singing Genes." Walter Cronkite's UNIVERSE. CBS-TV. New York. 3

August, 1982.

Palmer, Robert. "When Is It Rock and When Rock "N" Roll? A Critic Ventures an

Answer.." New York Times. 6 Aug. 1978: 14.

Smith, William. Dictionary of the Bible. Philadelphia: National. (n. d.)

Southern, Eileen. The Music of Black Americans. 2nd Ed. New York: Norton, 1983.

Task Force on the Philosophy of Music. Music—It's Role, Qualities, and Influence.

Washington, DC, GC of SDA, 1972

Titon, Jeff Todd, et al. Worlds of Music: An Introduction to the Music of the World's

Peoples. New York: Schirmer, 1984.

Torres, Louis R, and Carol A. Torres. Notes on Music.. Maries: LMN 19.

White, Ellen G. The Acts of the Apostles. Mountain View: Pacific, 1911.

---. The Adventist Home. Nashville: Southern, 1952.

---. Christ's Object Lessons. Washington, DC: Review, 1952.

---. Counsels on Diets and Foods. Takoma Park: Review, 1976.

---. Counsels to Parents and Teachers. Mountain View: Pacific, 1943.

---. The Desire of Ages. Silver Spring: Better Living, 1990.

---. Education. Boise: Pacific, 1952.

---. "Ellen G. White Comments." SDA Bible Commentary. Washington, DC: Review, 1955

---. Evangelism. Boise: Pacific, 1952.

---. The Great Controversy. Mountain View: Pacific, 1911.

---. Letter 6b, 1893.

---. Manuscript 33, 1886.

---. Our High Calling. Washington, DC: Review, 1961

---. Patriarchs and Prophets. Mountain View: Pacific, 1913.

---. Selected Messages. 3 vols. Washington, DC: Review, 1958.

---. The Southern Work. Washington, DC: Review, 1966

---. Steps to Christ. Washington, DC: Review, 1973.

---. Testimonies for the Church. 9 vols. Mountain View: Pacific, 1948.

---. That I May Know Him. Washington, DC: Review, 1964.

---. This Day with God. Washington, DC: Review, 1979.

Wilkerson, David. Set the Trumpet to Thy Mouth. Lindale: World, 1985.

INDEX

To receive *What God Says About Music,*
please write to:
AWSAHM MUSIC
P. O. 3586
Huntsville, AL 35810-3586

•

Dr. Eurydice V. Osterman is available
for music seminars. To contact her, write to the address
above or call 256-726-7281 (Work), 256-851-8513 (Home),
or 256-852-8100 (Fax). Email: eosterman@oakwood.edu
Please use the book title in the subject reference.